LOGOS AGAPE

GOD'S WONDERFUL STORY OF LOVE

BY

JOHN W. JENSEN

May God continue to Bless
you as you minister for Him
in Christ
John Jensen

LOGO'S AGAPE

GOD'S WONDERFUL STORY OF LOVE

By John W Jensen

About the Author

John, at the age of eighteen, gave his heart and life to Jesus Christ His Lord and Savior. Since that time he has diligently studied and taught the Word of God for a period of over fifty years. Having studied New Testament Greek and using His Greek New Testament and Hebrew sources He has been able under the guidance of the Holy Spirit of Truth to give in depth revelation of the many facets and unsearchable riches found in the Word of God.

This was written that the reader may know and receive Jesus as Lord and Savior and be edified (built up) through studying His Word, "For the perfecting of the Saints, for the work of the ministry, for the edifying of the body of Christ". He has the support of his dearly beloved wife of sixty some years, Joanne and his talented and lovely daughters; Melodie and Holly. And his son Jon Derek who is waiting in heaven for us all.

About the Book

Throughout the writing of this book "Logo's Agape", I have, under the guidance of the Holy Spirit endeavored to apply the Word of God in many different applications with emphasis on the thought and intent as it is defined by His Word. I have purposed within my heart to allow God to reveal Himself to you through this writing: His so great salvation; His grace; His provision and His loving-kindness through Jesus Christ His Son in the anointing power of His Holy Spirit. As you read this book, let the Holy Spirit have His way in revealing the mystery of His will to your heart and life.

Acknowledgements & Dedication

To my wife Joanne, whose love makes my life so very blessed;

To my daughter Melodie
Who takes me away bowling and shows no mercy;

To my daughter Holly
who took time from her own busy schedule
in Graphic Arts to design the cover of this book and
prepare it for production;

and to the memory of my beloved son,
Jon Derek, who has gone home to be with the Lord.
This book is dedicated to you, son. I miss you so very much,
but I know I will one day see you again.

Galatians 2:20

I have been crucified with Christ: nevertheless I live;
yet not I, but Christ lives in me: and the life which
I now live in the flesh I live by the faith of the
Son of God, Who loved me,and gave Himself for me.

Introduction to

Logo's Agape: God's Wonderful Story of Love

Hebrews 4:12 states, "For the Word of God is quick (alive, and Powerful and sharper than any two edged sword, piercing even to the dividing asunder of soul and spirit, and of the joints and marrow, and is a discerner of the thoughts and intent of the heart." The Word of God is Truth as Jesus Christ is the Word and Jesus is the Truth. I Timothy 3:16-17 further states, "All scripture (Word of God) is given by inspiration of God, and is profitable for doctrine, for correction, for instruction in righteousness: That the man of God may be perfect, thoroughly furnished unto all good works". The Word of God is referred to in Ephesians 6:17 as the "Sword of the Spirit". God proclaims in Isaiah 55:121, "So shall my Word be that goeth forth out of my mouth: it shall not return unto me void (empty without fruit) but it shall accomplish that which I please, and it shall prosper in the things whereto I sent it". Isaiah 1:18 invites everyone, "Come now and let us reason together, saith the Lord (the Word of Truth): though your sins be as scarlet, they shall be as white as snow; though they be red like crimson, they shall be as wool". For instance the Word found in John 3:16 "For God so loved the world that He gave His only begotten Son, that whosoever believeth in Him should not perish, but have everlasting life" when used by a man of God has various spiritual applications: God's love for His created beings; His faithfulness to us ward; and Everlasting life. God's Word is the breath of God poured out upon all flesh. II timothy 2:15 exhorts "Study (be diligent in meditation), to show thyself approved unto God, a workman that needeth not to be ashamed, rightly dividing the Word of Truth".

During this writing I have been in much prayer and supplication before God and wrote as I felt led of the Spirit. I am 87 years of age and have given all of my lifetime in the study and application of the Word of God. I studied Greek and used Hebrew concordances and writings extensively in my writing to know and understand the Wisdom of God in His Word of Power; in His intercourse and interaction with His people as recorded in the Old and New Testaments. It has become my life, "a lamp unto my feet, and a light unto my path" (Psalm 119:105). In all that I have written, taught and preached of the Word of God, I have found that He is the Rock of Ages; a sure foundation to all that trust Him.

Therefore, throughout this writing, I have, under the guidance of the Holy Spirit endeavored to apply the Word of God in many different applications with emphasis on the thought and intent as it is defined by His Word. I have purposed within my heart to allow God to reveal Himself to you through this writing: His so great salvation; His grace; His provision and His loving-kindness through Jesus Christ His Son in the anointing power of His Holy Spirit. As you read this book, let the Holy Spirit have His way in revealing the mystery of His will to your heart and life.

WONDERFUL STORY OF LOVE

TABLE OF CONTENTS

CHAPTER ONE

THE BIBLE - GOD'S REVELATION OF HIS LOVE

THE HISTORY OF MAN BEGINS WITH GOD'S LOVE

Of all of the books ever written, of all of the literature ever penned, of all of the critical historical explanations and analysis of mankind ever given, there is only one magnificent and historically true account and record of mankind that fully reveals the significance of the creation of man, of his beginning and end: The Holy Bible, the Word of God. Only God, Creator of this vast universe and especially this planet earth with its inhabitants, knew before He laid the foundations of the world, that He would create man and woman in His image. The essence of God is so filled with such love and desire that He in lovingkindness created a family upon whom He could bestow His Love and affection. He first created Adam and Eve with whom He could fellowship and bless with Himself. To manifest His so great love for His creation, as the Triune God (God the Father, and God the Son, and God the Holy Spirit) He created man in His Own mage and breathed into man's nostrils His Own breath (spirit) of life to create him a living soul, a spiritual being within a body of clay (flesh).

The Word reveals to us that God is Love. Everything about God is Holy (Pure) and Holy Love describes God in His creative fiat of man and woman and of the beasts and animals of the field and the fowls of the air and the creeping things of earth and the fish and other aquatic animals of the sea. Even the vast celestial heavens and space of the universe declare His glorious Love. The sun, moon, stars, celestial galaxies, the myriad of stars and the planets and other galactic ethereal bodies were made for man and as yet to be discovered by man. They are used in navigation, in exploration of space, in the seasons of sowing and reaping. Oh, God is so glorious and He made it all for you and me, because He loves us so.

The Word of God is unique in that it contains the very breath and Spirit of God and therefore speaks with the authority of God. Its power of Truth and Love reaches out to the heart and soul of mankind and when read and studied and diligently meditated upon it will enlighten and illuminate the mind of that soul thirsty to find and know God in all of His loving kindness. It will literally open spiritually blind eyes that they may clearly see the Truth and receive Wisdom and understanding as to the will of God for His creation in this present world. It is the will of God as manifested through His Word of Truth, that mankind, His creation should live in love and joy and peace or as our Constitution of the United States proclaims, to enjoy the fruits of life, liberty and the pursuit of happiness. Love did not create or cause the chaos in this world. For this to happen it took the brilliant but greedy and egotistical minds of mankind under the deceiving leadership of God's arch enemy, Satan. The destruction of God's original intent of blessing mankind with his benevolent Love was directly caused by those whom He created. Those who had decided to forget the Lord God Almighty, creator of this vast universe and have a narcissus opinion of them-selves.

GOD'S LOVE STORY REVEALED THROUGH HIS CREATION

The Word of God was written by human vessels of clay, individuals of all walks of life (kings, poets, princes, philosophers, prophets, statesmen, tax collector, religious leaders, preachers, fishermen, apostles, physician and a host of other diverse occupations) under the inspiration of God Himself through His Holy Spirit of Truth. Although God's Word was written by so many different writers with different characteristics, personalities and writing abilities, yet it is evident that the message is of one Mind, the Lord God Almighty given through the inspiration of His Holy Spirit of Truth. It was written by 40 authors over a period of 1600 years and God's message of love to His creation is contained in 66 books divided as the Old Testament (First Love Covenant of God-37 books) and New Testament (New Love Covenant of God-29 books). Throughout these holy writings there is one clear thread of unity of thought and purpose that reveals one omniscient author: Almighty God, Who is in Himself Divine Revelation. As recorded in Isaiah 55:11 God speaks concerning His Word of Truth, "So shall My Word be that goeth forth out of My mouth, it shall not return unto Me void, but it shall accomplish that which I please, and it shall prosper in the thing (that which belongs to God-His creation) whereto I send it".

This Book is a diversified and yet compact story of God's wonderful and everlasting Love for His created beings; who are made in His image and as His offspring will become by choice (as they with thankful hearts receive and experience His Love) His true family of Sons and Daughters through Jesus Christ His Son. The Bible, the Word of God bears God's stamp of Himself and reveals only that which the Lord God Almighty inspired to be written through His Holy Spirit of Truth. It is only what saith the Lord God Almighty.

The Bible is a self-contained exposition of God's love that is never out of date and has never lost its appeal for the masses of humanity regardless of the reasons for reading it's amazing and phenomenally accurate revelations and Divine Truth concerning the humanity of mankind. Within the front and back covers of this Spirit filled volume God reveals His story of love manifested in His creation of Adam and Eve and throughout the history of mankind from beginning to end. It is a Wonderful Story of Love: a story of time and eternity, eternity before and after the time of mankind here on earth. It reveals the omnipotence of God in His creative power, His presence here on earth demonstrated by His miracles and healing power and His resolve and redemptive reconciliation of His beloved created beings provided through Jesus Christ His Son as the Son of man. It reveals the omniscience of God in all of His creative design in the developmental stages of His object of His Love, mankind. The Love of God is evident in His creation of nature; of land masses; of His vast universe of the sun, moon and stars; of myriads of galaxies; of planets; meteors and all of the signs and wonders of space much of which has not even been remotely explored.

God is a God of order and purpose who has given to all who will read and know and understand what thus sayeth the Lord God Almighty concerning His creation including mankind: his present and future existence. In essence, the existence and future of mankind is predicated upon his response to such Love. This wonderful story of Love is a progressive story that begins with God's love manifested as He carefully chose the purest clay of his created earth and molded it tenderly and purposely with His powerful loving hands that the blueprint of His omniscient mind miraculously transformed into a beautiful body of flesh. God then quickened, made alive, this body of flesh (fashioned by God Himself) by the power of his breath (Spirit) of life and man became a living soul. In the beginning as it is today, it is God with us here on earth. In the eternity to come it will be we with God in His Glory forever and ever. So the Bible, the Word of God is His story predicated upon His will, His Word, His Messiah (Jesus His Son), His creative fiat, His works quickened by His dunamis, energo power of His Holy Spirit of Truth: His will.

CHAPTER TWO

THE SOURCE OF LOVE

GOD IS LOVE

The source of Love is the Lord God Almighty, the Most High God. He has communicated to His created beings this truth through His creation of the Universe; through His Word of Truth, the Holy Bible; though His Son, Jesus; and by His Holy Spirit of Truth. Thus, it is without doubt the most important book ever written because although it was written by human instrument, yet it is given through the inspiration of the Holy Spirit by God and the author of Truth and His Word of Truth, Jesus Christ His Son. It is God's own message to the world which God created and has revealed through His Son, the Word in the power of the Holy Spirit. The Bible reveals to His created beings the mystery, wisdom and wonder of His creative fiat, His plan that reveals His so great love for His created beings even before they knew Him as God and as our Father Who art in heaven. In essence the Bible is a story that reveals God Himself as Love. The Love of God that is the source of His creative fiat: of His offspring that would be made in His image and become His sons and daughters, His progeny of Love.

When one reads the Word of God, the Bible, it is evident that God's heart was so filled with His Holy Love as He began His creation of Adam and Eve that He must have thought, "How do I Love thee? Let me demonstrate the ways. I will first make you (man and women) in my image. I will breathe my breath of life into you (Adam and Eve) and make you a living soul possessed of a spirit capable of expressing the same quality of Love that I have bestowed upon you, my created beloved ones. I will take the clay from a special reserve of the earth that I created and with tender loving care work it lovingly with my own powerful hands and with a predetermined design mold it into a beautiful and magnificent creature that will be a reflection (image) of me with finite ability and power and resource. I will give you My

Word of Truth, My Everlasting Covenant that expresses My love for you and that cannot be broken. I will pour out My blessings upon you, My beloved creative children and give you eternal life. You shall be like Me, the Most High God".

ROOTED AND GROUNDED IN LOVE

When in college I read a poem by Elizabeth Barrett Browning concerning the one whom she so loved that she wrote the poem, "How do I love thee? Let me count the ways". Elizabeth Browning must have known the love of God personally as she used some of God's own words to express her feelings. She begins with, "I love thee to the depth and breadth and height my soul can reach". Paul prays for God's children as recorded in Ephesians 3:17-19, "That Christ may dwell in your hearts by faith; that ye, being rooted and grounded in love, May be able to comprehend with all saints what is the breadth, and length, and depth, and height; And to know the love of Christ, which passeth knowledge, that ye might be filled with all the fullness of God".

The word for rooted in the Greek is rhizkoo which refers to an offspring or progeny. It is the source of our English word rhizome or root from which a plant life grows. It is the dwelling place of a sprout as from a seed, the essence of life where it is nourished and established (substantiated) before it produces a sprout that breaks through the sod of earth and reaches with its leafy head toward heaven in newness of life. We are His offspring, made in the image of our God Who is Love. We are also grounded or built upon the ground or foundation of Jesus Christ the Lord, the Son of God, Who so loved us that He gave His Life that we may have Life everlasting, abundant and free. I Corinthians 3:11 affirms, "For (no) other foundation can no man lay than that is laid, which is Jesus Christ".

GOD'S WORD OF ETERNAL LOVE

There are not sufficient words of man's finite ability to fully express the Truth of God's Love as recorded in His Holy Word, The Bible. Therefore, let me repeat myself to clearly state God's story or revelation of His Love for His created beings. It is God's story or revelation of His supreme love for His children as manifested by His providential care, His provision for their redemption and reconciliation, for their nourishing and healing, for the preservation of their spirit, soul and body. It is a story of the revelation of God's love manifested throughout the ages of time and chronicled upon the pages of His Word of Truth. It is God's prophetic message of love in truth for the revelation of Himself to His children and their children's children. No other writing, no other book, no other treatise, no other essay or volumes of historical or religious content can equal the Bible, for it is the inspired Word of God. You only have to read it, meditate upon it, study it, and experience its revelation of Truth to know that it is truly what thus sayeth the Lord God Almighty. At the cross of Jesus, where Jesus body writhed in agony, His last drop of blood drained from His veins and His heart of Love pierced by a Roman spear, He said, "It is finished" and died, and the unbelieving Roman guard (Centurion) experiencing that moment of truth in his life fell on his knees and shouted in belief, "Truly this was the Son of God" (Matthew 27:50-54).

God's heart speaks of His love for His created beings in one stated revelation of Truth, "For God so loved the world that He gave His only begotten Son, what whosoever believeth in Him should not perish, but have everlasting life". Jesus said to His disciples in John 14:21 (NKJV), "He who has my commandments (Word of Truth), and keeps them, it is he who loves Me. And he who loves Me shall be loved of My Father, and I will love Him and will manifest (reveal) Myself to him".

CHAPTER THREE

MAN'S STORY OF LOVE WITHOUT GOD'S LOVE

MAN MADE THEORIES

God made man in His image and gave him life by breathing into His nostrils and making Him a living soul. Man's original nature was that of Love as he walked and talked with God in His beautiful Garden of Eden on a daily basis. Man knew about Love from God Himself. But man also had the divine power of the psyche or mind to think and reason and feel and choose and to reason, philosophize and create. Yes, man can mentally create with his God given ability in that he is able to form ideas and present them as fact and put them into operation whether right or wrong. Mankind or God's created beings of flesh and blood have over the ages of time and at various intervals lost their first love and devotion to God and sought to raise themselves up in power and position above Almighty God Himself. A very serious and studious undertaking although a most futile effort that spells doomsday from the start. For example: the Tower of Babel; the time of Noah and the flood; the various gods of the different ethnic tribes who connived and contrived to worship a god of their own choosing. Read the account of Elijah the man of God and the prophets of Baal recorded in I Kings Chapter 18.

The kingdoms and nations of this world since the early beginnings of man have felt a need to worship, but they wanted control over whom or what they worshipped, an oxymoron? Then there were those who felt a need to have or make many gods so as to meet every fearful problem or contingency they may encounter in life. They wanted to cover all bases so to speak. They made their own gods, with eyes that could not see and ears that could not hear and with mouths that could not speak, in other words deaf, dumb and mute. They wanted a god through which they could conger up imaginations and give them permission to utilize their selfish lusts such as gods of fertility with temples for prostitution and sacrificial murder to appease the gods (subconsciously, gratify themselves). They even sacrificed their own children to the god Moloch.

Even today they sacrifice their unborn babies to their god of lust and perverted desires by abortion.

Paul encountered a people of his day who had made unto themselves many gods or idols. In fact they even made an idol to an unknown God. The Apostle Luke wrote, "Now while Paul waited for them (his fellow companions) at Athens, his spirit was stirred in him, when he saw the city wholly given to idolatry" (Acts 17:16). "Then Paul stood in the midst of Mars Hill (the Areopagus), and said, 'ye men of Athens, I perceive that in all things ye are too superstitious (very religious). For as I passed by, and beheld your devotions, I found an altar with this inscription, 'To the unknown god', whom therefore ye ignorantly (without knowing) worship, Him declare I unto you. God that made the world and all things therein and earth, dwells not in temples made with hands; Neither is worshiped with men's hands, as though He needed anything, seeing He giveth to all life, and breath, and all things; And hath made of one blood all nations of men to dwell on all the face of the earth, and hath determined the times before appointed, and the bounds of their habitation; That they should seek the Lord, if haply they might feel after Him, and find Him, though He not be far from every one of us. For in Him we live, and move, and have our being; as certain also of your own poets have said, for we are also His offspring. Forasmuch then as we are the offspring of God we ought not to think that the Godhead (Divine Nature in three persons) is like unto gold, or silver, or stone, graven by art and man's device (devising). And the times of this ignorance God winked at (overlooked); but now commanded all men everywhere to repent" (Acts 17:22-30). It is time for the world to grow up and put away childish things and acknowledge the Truth concerning the Lord God Almighty.

The God Who made us knows what is in the mind of man. Isaiah 55:8 reveals, "For My (God's) thoughts are not your thoughts, neither are your ways my ways, saith the Lord". Therefore a man or woman who rejects the Truth of the Word of God and proclaims "No God for me" is left to their own finite ways and stratagems to contemplate and idealize. When they are confident that they have sufficient reason to proceed further (by their own finite minds) they fashioned for themselves with their own hands or minds, idols which they worshipped as gods. I say idols or minds because although still in practice today, initially man made with his own hands idols to worship. However, over the last century and perhaps somewhat before, man has made for himself and for all those who will be deceived, idols (with the help of evil spirits): conjured up grotesque images to worship: Manmade ideas, thoughts and theories whereby they postulate that there is no God and that they are a god unto themselves (what a horrible thought). As recorded in the period of the judges (Judges 21:25) "every man did that which was (seemed) right in his own eyes". The eyes of mankind without the knowledge and wisdom of God is capable of unimaginable atrocities perpetrated upon mankind even to the annihilation of a people, perverted conduct and malevolent behavior.

MAN'S CONCEITED THEORY OF EVOLUTION

Thus, a fragment of an ancient relic, the bones of a long departed animal or man (who was created by God) are pieced together from various areas of the earth, given high sounding names and passed off as man's answer to God's creative fiat under the guise of man's own contrived theory of evolution. The Beagle (Freud's craft) must have lost its scent due to the saltiness of the sea air. I studied evolution and various other anthropological theories in college and came away feeling that the human race must have missed a turn somewhere in their analysis of the beginning of life. In their eagerness to disassociate themselves from God and reject His wisdom and truth in God's creative universe they have egregiously wandered out into no man's land of ambiguity and witchcraft. Even greater an error of humanity is that there are those who will believe such nonsense and spend a lifetime of studying and traveling to various parts of the earth to dig up the dead artifacts of ages past and reevaluate them in the light of their newly found intellect (the one with the loose screw). They evaluate and sort into neat categories and with finite minds void of the truth, present their own theories about nothing. Oh, the volumes of books and the millions of hours of wasted time and energy of well-meaning students of our colleges and universities with their prestigious degrees in pursuit of their meaningless accomplishments. I am not necessarily speaking of those well-meaning individuals who willingly are followers of the blind, but to the perpetrators, those long deceased and those of today who have and are now knowingly continuing their propagation of a fatal lie.

Enough said, and if you disagree that is your prerogative, but if you are searching for the truth of the matter than consult the Book that God wrote concerning his wonderful story of love in creation. It will stand the test of time and eternity. God even gives His word of Truth in addressing this fiasco of evolution found in Romans 1:18-23, "For the wrath of God is revealed from heaven against all ungodliness and unrighteousness of men, who hold the truth in unrighteousness; Because that which may be known of God is manifest (evident) in them: for God hath showed it unto them. For the invisible things of Him from the creation of the world are clearly seen, being understood by the things that are made, even His eternal power and Godhead, so that they are without excuse. Because that, when they knew God, they glorified Him not as God, neither were thankful, but became vain in their imaginations, and their foolish heart was darkened. Professing their selves to be wise, they became fools, and changed the glory of the uncorruptible God into an image made like to corruptible (perishing) man, and to birds, and four-footed beasts, and creeping things".

The media will reveal little of the infighting and differences of opinion and failures of dating devises such as the carbon test and a multiplied number of other mythical projects in their never ending quest to prove something that cannot be proven, the beginning and evolution of man without God.

In the perfection and beauty of their creative design, all of nature cries out that there is a Creator God of heaven and earth. Just look at all of nature and our vast universe of sun, moon and stars and the rotation of the earth with its effects on the tides and the seasons. Just look at man and woman, the intricate detail of their brain that controls their various body systems that operate together with such precision and in such detail that only the Lord God Almighty by His omnipotent omniscience could design such a fabulous and marvelous creation. Just consider for a moment that part of man that has baffled science throughout the ages, the spirit and soul of man that God's Word reveals came from God Himself. Many of the scientific community today believe that there is an element within man that is a mystery to them as to how it operates in his life. Some call it a spiritual force that seems to be an intricate part of the life of man beyond that of his physical body.

THE HISTORICAL PERPETRATOR OF MANS ARROGANCE

The spiritual evil force in this world which operates against man and which is behind his pursuit for power and control of the universe without God is the one and only original arch enemy of God, Satan. He himself is a created being, created by God as one of God's highest angels, an Arch Angel to be His bearer of Light in Worshiping the Most High God. He was called Lucifer (day star) originally an obedient angelic creation of God who because of his iniquity, his lust of the flesh and his pride of life (haughty spirit) rebelled against God. Isaiah 14:12-17 records God's scathing indictment of Satan's boastful heart of pride, "How art thou fallen from heaven, O Lucifer, son of the morning! How art thou cut down to the ground (thrown out of heaven to earth), which did weaken the nations! For thou hast said in thine heart, I will ascend into heaven, I will exalt my throne above the stars of God, I will sit also upon the mount of the congregation, in the sides of the north (Gods personal dwelling place). I will ascend above the heights of the clouds; I will be like the most High (God). Yet thou shalt be brought down to hell, to the sides of the pit. They that see thee shall narrowly look upon (gaze at) thee, and consider thee, saying, Is this the man that made the earth to tremble, that did shake kingdoms; That made the world as a wilderness, and destroyed the cities thereof; that opened not the house of his prisoners?" In essence it is Satan's control of certain individuals with evil hearts and minds that deceives and destroys. The enslaving political ideologies of this world such as communism and man contrived religious elements of this world are manmade devices for the despotic conquest, murder and destruction of the people of this world by Satan controlled madmen who deceive the masses by appealing to their lustful appetites.

I John 2:15-17 records God's revelation concerning the iniquity of Satan, "Love not the world, neither the things that are in the world. If any man loves the world, the love of the Father is not in him. For all that is in the world, the lust of the flesh, and the lust of the eyes, and the pride of life, is not of the Father, but is of the world. And the world passeth away, and the lust thereof; but he that doeth the will of God abideth forever". Because Satan (adversary) deceived one-third of the angels of heaven, Satan and his demon angels were cast out of God's heavenly domain down to earth seething with anger and despising God, using his (Satan's) power of lying deceit to damn God's beloved creation to join him in his God appointed abode in hell. The Word of God identifies Satan: as the originator of sin, "He that committeth sin is of the devil; for the devil sinneth from the beginning. For this purpose the Son of God was manifested, that He might destroy the works of the devil" (I John 3:8); as "that wicked (evil, immoral) one", "He that is begotten of God (has made Jesus Lord and Savior of his life) keeps (lives and walks in the Holy Spirit) himself , and that wicked one touches him not" I John 5:18; a thief and destroyer of all those who he has duped and deceived, "The thief (Satan) cometh not, but for to steal, and to kill, and to destroy; I (Jesus) am come that they (God's created beings) might have life, and that they might have it more abundantly" (John 10:10); a deceiver, "And the great dragon was cast out, that old serpent, called the Devil, and Satan, which deceives the whole world; he was cast out into the earth, and his angels were cast out with him" (Revelations 12;9); a murderer and liar, " You are of your father the devil, and the lusts of your father you will do. He was a murderer from the beginning, and abode not in the truth, because there is no truth in him. When he speaks a lie, he speaks of his own; for he is a liar, and the father of it" (John 8:44); the accuser of the brethren (children of God), " And I heard a loud voice saying in heaven, 'Now is come salvation, and strength, and the kingdom of our God, and the power of His Christ; for the accuser of our brethren (Satan) is cast down, which accused them (children of God) before our God day and night'" (Revelations 12:10).

CHAPTER FOUR

GOD'S STORY OF LOVE FROM THE BEGINNING

GENESIS: THE BIRTH OF BEGINNINGS

God's written Love story begins with the book of Genesis (book of beginnings) and reveals God's Love in His interaction with His first family of record, Adam and Eve and their offspring and future generations. Thus it is the beginning of the human race; the beginning of family life and early civilization; the beginning of the formation of the nations of the world and His chosen people, the Hebrew race and the Church family of God. Because of Satan, God's adversary and arch enemy, it is also the beginning of conflict and lawlessness, disobedience (sin) against God. Therefore it is also a time of the absence of Love among men. However, God has never stopped loving his beloved creation and is always mindful of them. In spite of their disobedience and even rejection, yet He diligently strives to keep them in the fold of His heart (in the cleft of the Rock of Ages) through His promise of reconciliation, of redemption and restoration and resurrection for whosoever will hear Him call "come unto Me" and receive Jesus His only begotten Son, as Lord and Savior.

The Biblical account, God's Word of Truth, reveals God's prescribed pattern of historic genealogy through the hierarchy of His chosen people, His elect the Hebrew race. Within this human nuclei of God's own choosing, God laid the foundation of faith and hope and love. God's love is manifested in all of his works for and in His creation including mankind. God made man and in His Image, a spirit being with a soul as God breathed into man's nostril and man became a spirit being with a living soul. He also made for man a body of flesh which He formed from the clay of the earth. God made man with all of the necessary physical, mental, emotional and spiritual components. The soul of man although finite (having bounds or limitations, not infinite as God) coexists with a never dying spirit. The soul of man consists of the attributes of will, sense, feeling, ability to think and to know and to mentally create, with the ability to decide, choose, calculate, analyze, including the ability to think and to reason and to define, yes and the ability to believe for God in His creative fiat has given man His initial portion or measure of faith.

God created for man a magnificent body that is able to perform an exhausting list of useful tasks, physically, mentally, emotionally and spiritually. It is evident by the word of God that man's body is unique as a means of mobility with the capability of self-maintenance by the consumption of nutrients (food staples and liquids) necessary for growth and health. The skeletal frame is uniquely formed of bones to which are attached muscles and sinews and ligaments and flesh. It has a circulatory system in which a muscular organ, the heart, that rhythmically pumps blood through various sizes of connecting blood vessels or veins through which flow life giving nutrients, oxygen and hormones to various parts of the body and waste material to the excretory organs. It has a well-designed pulmonary or breathing system of lungs, mouth and nose, a unique digestive system, an adrenaline system and a digestive system. Although God made man a living soul that functions as the mind of the spirit of man yet God made man a brain of flesh that is responsible for the interpretation of sensory impulses of the body (impulses and direction for health and well-being to all parts of the body) and for the coordination and control of bodily activities and the exercise of emotion and thought of the body. For protection of two vital organs, God put man's heart of flesh in a protective rib cage and the vulnerable brain he encased in a skull of interlocking bone fragments.

Oh how marvelous, how wonderfully we as God's creation are made. David in his time, not knowing about all the wonderful advancements that science has given mankind concerning the delicate and intricate yet strong and durable makeup of the body of man wrote, "I will praise Thee (God); for I am fearfully (reverential awe) and wonderfully made: marvelous are Thy works; and that my soul knoweth right well (of your goodness and loving kindness). My substance (frame) was made in secret (it was a time that God so loved He made man with only Himself, His Son Jesus and the Holy Spirit as witnesses), and curiously wrought in the lowest parts of the earth. Thine eyes did see my substance, yet being unperfect (not completely formed); and in Thy book all my members were written, which in continuance were fashioned (the days fashioned for me), when as yet there was none of them" (Psalm 139:14-16). To understand a more in depth rendition of these versus in the Amplified Bible we read, "I will confess and praise You for You are fearful (awesome) and wonderful and for the awful (awesome) wonder of my birth! Wonderful are Your works; and that my inner self knows right well. My frame was not hidden from You when I was being formed in secret (and) intricately and curiously wrought (as if embroidered with various colors) in the depths of the earth (a region of secrecy and mystery)".

THE BEGINNING OF GOD'S LAW OF OBEDIENCE AND WORSHIP

To begin with, God made man in His image (a reflection of God in finite attributes and abilities). When we make a comparison of the attributes of God with the abilities of His creation: in man we see a distinction between his human, finite abilities compared with God's infinite Divine nature. Man receives his knowledge from Almighty God, but man's knowledge is finite and limited, God is infinitely Omniscient (all knowing). Man is able to present himself in numerable operations of life, one at a time only. God is Omnipresent (present at all times everywhere (God fills the universe with His presence). Man has been given power to exercise over all the earth, but God is Omnipotent (all powerful). Therefore, although man possesses the attributes and abilities of God as a finite being, man is still dependent upon God for all that he is, all that he has in this present world and all that he will have, as promised by God, in the eternity to come.

The Word is clear in its revelation that God knows all about us. As put in the vernacular of today, God knows what makes us tick. Therefore, God knew that man needed Laws by which to govern himself for the peace and tranquility of the people, a uniform set of laws that would cover every aspect of human interaction and endeavor in a just and equitable way for the wellbeing of all the people.

God's original Ten Commandments concerning man's relationship with God and with each other is a pattern for our conduct and worship before God and for the benefit and posterity of mankind. Exodus chapter twenty says that God spake unto the people: Thou shalt not make unto thee any graven image; thou shalt not bow down or serve any idol as a god; Thou shalt not take the name of the Lord thy God in vain; Remember the Sabbath day, to keep it holy; Honor thy father and thy mother; Thou shalt not kill; Thou shalt not steal; Thou shalt not bear false witness against thy neighbor. Thou shalt not covet (an unhealthy and lawless desire (lust) or craving for something that belongs to someone else).

From the beginning, even when sin entered into His Garden of Eden, God had already predestined His created beings to live in the glory of His presence through His Son Jesus, His gift of love. Knowing that He gave to man the awesome responsibility to make proper choices, he knew that the deceiver of mankind, Satan would with vengeance endeavor to interfere with God's original plan for His created man and woman. He knew before the foundations of the world that His love for His creation would necessitate that He manifest Himself through His Messiah, His only begotten Son Jesus. He gave us His Word of hope in the beginning. Ephesians 1:4-6 states, "According as He hath chosen us in Him before the foundations of the world, that we should be holy and without blame before Him in Love. Having predestinated us unto the adoption of children (as sons) by Jesus Christ to Himself, according to the good pleasure of His will, To the praise of the glory of His grace, wherein He hath made us accepted in the Beloved (Jesus)". Then in Romans 8:29-30, "For whom (His created beings) (He (God) did foreknow He also did predestinate to be conformed to the image of His Son (Jesus) that He (Jesus) might be the first born among many brethren . Moreover whom He did predestinate, , them He also called : and whom He called, them He also justified; and whom He justified, them He also glorified."

The Greek word used her for predestinate is proorizo which means to ordain at a predetermined time or to appoint or choose the criteria to be used. It come from pro, a primary Greek preposition which means a time prior or before something is accomplished (at the beginning), and orizo which means to appoint or specify, to determine, in this case to determine before the foundation of the world was laid. Before creation God had determined that those who will to receive God's plan of salvation through Jesus Christ His Son shall become His (God's) adopted sons and daughters. Predestination is God's foreknowledge (His

Omniscience) of what He knew would happen in the Garden of Eden by the unwarranted choices of Adam and Eve and His plan of Redemption and reconciliation through Jesus Christ His Son to bring whosoever will believe and receive Him; Jesus, into a special relationship of restoration with Himself.

Oh, such Love, such wondrous Love. Just think about it! The love of God reached out to mankind even before we were created and foreordained, appointed and predestinated us to become His sons and daughters in the lifetime He has given us. God said in His Word that when He in essence foreknew us because He designed us and created us in His image, God knew also that the vessels of clay that He made in His image would be marred by sin because of His and mankind's arch enemy, Satan. God had already in His Omniscience prepared a place for us that where He is we may be also. He revealed through Jesus Christ His Son as the Son of man the Way, the Truth and the Life that He would preserve us until that day of glorification, that where He is we may be also. Paul prayed, "And the very God of peace sanctify you wholly; and I pray God your whole spirit, soul and body be preserved blameless unto the coming of our Lord Jesus Christ (I Thessalonians 5:23). There is none like unto our God

LOVE SO AMAZING

But it's all because of His wonderful Love that He planned and bestowed His Gracious Lovingkindness upon us. It is love Divine (God is Love), all loves excelling: Who foreknew us; Who predestined (chose) us as His own; Who created us; Who called us from among the unbelieving world, reconciled us back to Himself when we were lost in sin; Who redeemed us (forgave us of our transgressions); Who lifted us up out of the miry clay of sin and guilt; Who called us out of darkness into His marvelous light; Who sat us upon the Solid Rock of our Salvation (Jesus Christ our Lord and Savior) and established our life of faith; Who has written down our name in His Book of Life; Who sanctified us through His Word of Truth; Who filled us with His Holy Spirit of Truth; Who protects us, heals us, prospers us, is ever present with us. He (God) never leaves us alone, hears and answers our prayers, gives us peace that passes all understanding and joy unspeakable and full of glory. Our loving

God gives us strength when we are weak; Who's Grace is sufficient for our every need; Who has prepared for us a place (mansion) next to His (God's) own mansion on High and Who will give to us a glorified body and His promise (written with the blood of our Faithful Witness of God's Oath, Jesus Christ His Son) that we shall reign with Him as Kings and Priests over all the earth in the Millennial Reign of Christ and in the eternity to come. PRAISE THE LORD GOD ALMIGHTY!!! The destructive forces of this world today may fume and fuss and threaten God's people and in their futile efforts try to obliterate everything that pertains to Jesus Christ His Son and perpetrate their evil efforts to terrorize the Church, but the Word of Truth loudly proclaims above the world's uproar, Child of God, "And when these things begin to come to pass, then look up, and lift up you heads, for your redemption draweth nigh"!!. It is even at the door!!

THE LOVE OF GOD IS RICH AND PURE

No wonder the Love of God is called rich and pure and measureless and strong. It reaches out into His whole universe and everywhere you look you see His loving handiwork. God's Love is beyond description. If every one of His created beings were amanuenses (scribes) by trade; and if they could use the entire panorama of God's created and glorious and vast heavenly expanse as an ethereal tablet; and if every stock on earth were made into a writing instrument: to write about the Love of God would exhaust all of the effort of the scribes, all of the writing materials and all of the space of the heavens and still not accurately nor completely record such Love of God.

God's love is Omnipresent; there is no escaping His Love. The Psalmist David wrote, "Whither shall I go from thy Spirit (His Love, for God is Spirit and God is Love)? Or whither shall I (can I) flee from Thy presence? If I ascend up into heaven, Thou art there: If I make my bed in hell (Sheol-place of the dead), behold Thou art there. If I take the wings of the morning, and dwell in the uttermost parts of the sea; even there shall Thy hand lead me, and Thy right hand shall hold me (close to His heart of Love). If I say, surely the darkness shall cover me (fall on me); even the night shall be Light about me. Yea the darkness hides not from Thee; but the night shineth as the day: the darkness and the Light are both alike to Thee" (Psalm 138:7-12). God's so great Love is rich in that it is sumptuously (lavishly or unable to exhaust its supply) luxurious and abundantly (without measure) bountiful and fertile, fruitful and strong. There is nothing that can prevent God from exercising His manifestation of Love toward and for us (except our unwillingness to believe) and with Joy receive Him as our Lord and our God and Jesus as Lord and Savior and His precious Holy Spirit our Guiding Light of Truth within us. Jesus said on several occasions during His ministry here on earth that in some places and cities He could not perform the works of His Father, God, because of their unbelief. Believing Him opens the gates of heaven, opens our spiritual eyes to the Truth and makes it possible for God to pour out a blessing that we are not able to contain.

There is no measuring of God's Love expressed to us from before the foundation of this world was laid, throughout our lifetime and throughout eternity to come. As God is the same yesterday, today and forever, so is His Love toward His creation, mankind. He is neither partial to no one nor anyone; everyone who comes to Him in faith is in no wise cast out. Jesus said in Matthew 11:28-30, "Come unto Me all ye that labor and are heaven laden and I will give you rest. Take my yoke upon you, and learn of Me; for I am meek and lowly in heart, and you shall find rest unto your souls. For my yoke is easy, and my burden is light".

GOD'S AMAZING LOVE IN HIS AMAZING GRACE

One facet of the Amazing Love of God is His Amazing Grace, an outpouring of His compassionate mercy. The Hebrew word is hesed or the lovingkindness of God. Think about this for a moment. God created a spirit being in His image (man and woman) and endowed them with all of the finite characteristic attributes of a God Himself. He places them in His beautifully created environment and gives them dominion and power to explore it and subdue it and build upon it. God has given them wisdom and understanding and ability to be creative in their quest and cause the land to prosper and grow and yield various kinds of grains and fruits and vegetables. He made them caretakers of His vast creation, earth and caused them to multiply what God had originally created and to expand upon Gods created work though their God given strength, ingenuity and intellect.

God only asks of His created beings to be obedient to His Word of Truth which is given for their health and well-being. To satisfy their inward desire to praise and worship Him, God initially instituted the tabernacle as a place of worship where God's presence would be known and then God Himself visited His creation and through the virgin birth of Jesus Christ (God's Messiah) as the Son of man. After Jesus suffered, bled and died for the sins of mankind, He was resurrected and sent His Holy Spirit to be in and with them. As His Temple, the temple of the Holy Spirit we experience God and Jesus Christ His Son as the Holy Spirit is the Spirit of God and of Jesus Christ His Son. The Holy Spirit in us is Christ in us our Hope of Glory. Jesus is our assurance that we shall live in glory with Him forevermore.

God gives to us His Word of Truth and Righteousness and Words of Wisdom and understanding that if obeyed would bring us health and prosperity and a life that is abundant and free and worth the living. Through His inspired Word we receive His righteous instruction that is profitable for our reproof, our correction and edification that we may stand before Him perfect (mature in the fullness of Christ in us), thoroughly furnished unto all good works.

God has created us with a measure of His faith (the power to unite us with God unto all pleasing) that enables us to believe in Him and receive from Him all of the vast riches of His glory that He so desires to pour out upon us abundantly. But we must believe with all that is within us, without wavering and without any reservations, but to wholly trust Him, knowing without a shadow of doubt that He is Who He reveals to us that He is and know in Whom we have believed. We must believe to the extent that we trust in the Lord with all of our heart and not lean to our own understanding, but in all our ways acknowledge Him. Acknowledge Him as our Lord God creator whose goodness showers us daily with His benefits of His grace. I Colossians 1:10 exhorts us, "That ye might walk worthy of the Lord unto all pleasing, being fruitful in every good work, and increasing in the knowledge of God".

Ephesians 1:7 states, "In Whom (Jesus) we have redemption (from sin and its effects) through His blood, the forgiveness of sins, according to the riches of His grace". His Grace and tender mercies and forgiveness are all a part of His Love. The wonderful thing about it is that you can't earn God's Love, it is freely given.

We are being constantly beset with trials and persecutions and tribulations from numerous attacks of Satan and somehow through all of this some may be led to believe what I have been revealing through His word of truth about God's love for us and victory in Jesus is not fully attainable in this life. I realize that sometimes it is not easy to fully understand or comprehend what is ours in Christ Jesus our Lord, but by faith we can enter into His rest fully. By faith we are able to live a life of holiness that is pleasing unto God. By faith we can overcome all of the fiery darts (poison arrows) of Satan: sickness; disease, oppressing problems; difficult situations; tormenting demon enemies of the mind, soul and spirit; and the list is inexhaustible. Of a Truth I say unto you, by faith we have full and complete victory in Jesus. It is a matter of Proverbs 3:5-7, "Trust in the Lord with all of thine heart; and lean not unto your own understanding. In all of your ways acknowledge Him, and He shall direct your path. Be not wise in your own eyes: fear the Lord, and depart from evil".

It is a matter of committing everything to Him, submitting to Him, delighting in Him and resting in Him. I am no longer my own, for with a price I have been bought. I have crucified myself with Him on His cross and it is no longer I, but Christ in me my Hope of Glory. Few achieve living in the secrete place of the Most High God. But to live the abundant life, to be free indeed, to receive power to heal the sick, cast own demons, to do the greater things promised by the Father through Jesus Christ our Lord and enjoy fully the benefits that His so great salvation brings, then we must follow Him explicitly, without reservation having our mind stayed (established) on and in Him.

CHAPTER FIVE

GOD'S LOVE REVEALED IN AND THROUGH HIS WORD

GOD'S WORD – A REVELATION OF HIS LOVE

God's Word is freely given and revealed to His creation, mankind: by His written testimony; by His Inspiration through His Holy Spirit of Truth; by His spoken Word; through the person of His only begotten Son, Jesus Christ the Lord (The Word of God). It is God's revelation of His Love to His beloved creation. Hereby God reveals Himself to us: in all that He is "I AM THAT I AM"; in all of His personal attributes and power; in His Omnipotent, Omniscient and His Omnipresence; by His Lovingkindness, Mercy and grace; Through His forgiveness, reconciliation and restoration. Our Lord God Almighty dwells in the presence of His entire universe and especially in the hearts (spirit) of His dearly beloved vessels of clay.

His plan for His beloved created beings was designed before the foundation of the world was laid. His creative fiat meticulously and skillfully wrought and brought forth His special creation, Adam and eve and their progeny. His blueprint was His eternal pattern of the first cause and object of His Love, mankind. Since God is Love, what God conceived in His mind concerning His plans for His created beings was His thoughts, His design that came from His heart of Love.

The whole idea of God's Love toward His creation (mankind) is summed up in I John 4:7-12, "Beloved, let us love one another for love is of God; and everyone that loves is born of God, and knows God. He that loves not knows not God; for God is love. In this was manifested the love of God toward us, because that God sent His only begotten Son into the world, that we might live through Him. Herein is love, not that we loved God, but that He loved us, and sent His Son to be the propitiation for our sins. Beloved, if God so loved us we ought also to love one another. No man hath seen God at any time (physically). If we love one another, God dwells in us, and His love is perfected in us". The Greek word for propitiation is hilasmos which means that the shed blood and death of Jesus satisfied God's wrath pronounced upon all sin. He died in our stead as the Son of man. He became our scape goat by which we are reconciled back to God and cleansed from all our sins. The cover of the Ark of the Covenant or Mercy Seat is called hilastarios. Once a year under the Mosaic ordinances of worship the High Priest would kill one goat and sprinkle the blood on the Mercy Seat (represents Jesus substitutionary death for us) and the other goat was sent out into the desert (the carrying away of our sins). Thus man is justified as his sins are expiated (atoned for). Such is the wondrous Love God manifested through His Son Jesus. Love is not only an attribute of God, but it is His essence. He is LOVE Divine and the source of all true Love (All loves excelling).

The central thought in the heart of God is summed up in John 3:16, "For God so loved he world that He gave His only begotten Son, that whosoever believeth in Him should not perish, but have everlasting life". Jesus is God's Gift of Love to His created children of His love. In a sense we are His children by His creative fiat, made in His presence, formed by His hands, made in His image, given God's own breathe of life. However, since sin contaminated the human race, it was necessary that we become a new creation, children of His Love through the blood sacrifice of His Son, Jesus. When we receive Jesus as Lord and Savior we are adopted into God's Family and we become the sons and daughters of God. The bondage of sin has been destroyed. Romans 8:15-16 says it plainly, "For ye have not received the spirit of bondage (of sin) again to fear; but ye have received the Spirit of adoption, whereby we cry, 'Abba, Father'. The Spirit itself bears witness with our spirit, that we are the children of God".

THE COMMANDMENT OF LOVE AND THE LAW AND THE PROPHETS

Through His ordained Prophets of the Old Testament and the Law, God gave instruction to His people to keep and obey His law for life and prosperity. The breaking of His Law brought sin and judgment. His Law and subsequent laws were administered by His Priests. Prophets and Kings and addressed the cultural, social and spiritual aspects of Hebrew life. Jesus, God's ultimate Word of Truth came to show His Father to us and reveal to us a new law, that of Love. In John 13:34-35 Jesus tells

His disciples, "A new commandment I give unto you, That ye love one another; as I have loved you, that ye also love one another. By this shall all men know that ye are my disciples, if ye have love one to (for) another". Recorded in Mark 12:30-31 are these words of Jesus quoted from the Old Testament (Deuteronomy 10:12; 30:6 Leviticus 19:18, "'and thou shalt love the Lord thy God with all thy heart, and with all thy soul, and with all thy mind, and with all thy strength: this is the first commandment. And the second is like, namely this, Thou shalt love thy neighbor as thyself'. There is none other commandment greater than these". Matthew records the same two great commandments of God, but adds, "On these two commandments hang all the law and the prophets. The Love of God shed abroad in our hearts and demonstrated to our neighbors in longsuffering (merciful patience), gentleness, goodness and meekness fulfills all of the requirements of the Law. There is no greater Law than that of genuine Love (read I Corinthians 13:1-13).

Speaking in Ezekiel about the restoration of Israel Ezekiel 36:26 says, "A new heart also will give you, and a new spirit will I put within you and I will take away the stony heart out of your flesh and I will give you a heart of flesh". The Law of the Lord God was perfect, but mankind was not, but weak in the flesh (prone to wander) and without God's Holy Spirit unable to keep the Law in its entirety. Remember, the breaking of any part of the Law made one guilty of all. Romans 8:2-3 in speaking of the Law of the Spirit of Life in Christ Jesus said, "For what the law could not do, in that it was weak through the flesh, God sending His own Son in the likeness of sinful flesh, and for sin, condemned sin in the flesh: That the righteousness of the law might be fulfilled in us, who walk not after the flesh, but after the Spirit". The Law of God was good and perfect, man was not in that he was prone to disobey and sin against God.

The Psalmist David wrote in Psalm 19:7, "The Law of the Lord is perfect, converting the soul". Jesus said in Matthew 5:17 "Think not that I am come to destroy the law, or the prophets, I am not come to destroy, but to fulfill". The Law of the Spirit of Life in Christ Jesus goes deeper into the heart of the matter in the fulfilling of the Law. The Law says thou shalt not kill, but the Spirit speaks, do not be angry at your brother or sister, but Love them thus disarming the evil emotion to hate and the urge to kill. The Law says, thou shalt not commit adultery, but the Spirit says the lust of the flesh is the temptation that causes this sin. Love them in the Lord. The Law says, no divorce but Spirit says commit yourself unto God (and your spouse) and thereby not commit unrighteousness. The Law says we are not to take an oath, but the Spirit says speak the truth. The Law says, no retaliation, but the Spirit says, forgive your brother or sister seventy times seven if necessary, out of a heart of love. We are even to love our enemies as ourselves and pray for those who spitefully use us.

Galatians 5:14 reveals, "for all the law is fulfilled in one word, even in this; Thou shalt love thy neighbor as thyself'. The word says that love covers a multitude of sins, "And above all things have a fervent love among yourselves: for love shall cover a multitude of sins" (I Peter 4:8). It prevents them from being committed, from happening. How can you truly kill, steal from, lie to, or covet the possessions of those whom you truly and genuinely love in the Spirit? How can you dishonor your parents if you love them? How can you not serve God and keep His commandments if you truly love Him? Romans 13:8-10 explains, "Owe no man anything, but to love one another: for he that loves another has fulfilled the law. For this, 'Thou shalt not commit adultery, thou shalt not kill (murder), thou shalt not steal, thou shalt not bear false witness, thou shalt not covet; and if there be any other commandment, it is briefly comprehended in this saying, namely, thou shalt love thy neighbor as thyself'. Love worketh no ill (does no harm) to his neighbor: therefore, love is the fulfilling of the law".

THE LAW AND SIN

Paul is very methodical and meticulous in his presentation in Romans. He deals with the question of Justification or the imputation of righteousness. He then proceeds to the universal provision of righteousness and Justification of the law touching in particular upon Justification under the Law of the Old Testament. Beginning with Chapter Six and extending through Chapter Seven, Paul deals with freedom from sins power and the impartation of Righteousness. The new principle of sanctification is manifested in and through the person of Jesus Christ our righteousness. The new relationship in sanctification is emancipation from the law of sin and death. The power of sanctification is the work of the Holy Spirit within us. Christ in us the Hope of Glory.

There is no doubt about it concerning the holiness of the Law. Romans 7:12 confirms, "Wherefore the Law is Holy, and the commandment Holy, and just, and good". Romans 7:7-11 reveals the problem of indwelling sin, "What shall we say then? Is the law sin? God forbid. I had not known sin, but by the law: for I had not known lust except the law had said,'Thou halt not covet'. But sin taking occasion (opportunity) by the commandment (Law), wrought in me all manner of concupiscence (evil desire). For without (apart from) the law sin was dead". There is no sin imputed when there is no Law. "For I was alive without the law once; but when the commandment came, sin revived, and I died". For the wages of sin is death, therefore we are the living dead until we are revived by His Spirit. "And the commandment which was ordained to life, I found to be unto death. For sin, taking occasion by the commandment, deceived me, and by it slew me".

THE LAW AND OUR TWO NATURES

The struggle of man's two natures is well expressed in the Amplified Bible Romans 7:12-25. "The Law therefore is holy and (each) commandment is holy and just and good. Did that which is good then prove fatal (bringing death) to me? Certainly not! It was sin, working death in me by using this good thing (the Law as a weapon), in order that through the commandment sin might be shown up clearly to be sin, that the extreme malignity and immeasurable sinfulness of sin might plainly appear. We know that the Law is spiritual; but I am a creature of the flesh (carnal, unspiritual), having been sold into slavery under (the control of) sin. For I do not understand my own actions (I am baffled, bewildered). I do not practice or accomplish what I wish, but I do the very thing that I loathe (which my moral instinct condemns). Now if I do (habitually) what is contrary to my desire, (that means that) I acknowledge and agree that the Law is good (morally excellent) and that I take sides with it. However, it is no longer I who do the deed, but the sin (principle) which is at home in me and has possession of me". Verses 18-20 reveal the struggle to do that which is good in our spirit against the evil desire of our flesh. Then beginning with verse 21, "So I find it to be a law (rule of action of my being) that when I want to do what is right and good, evil is ever present with me and I am subject to its (sins) insistent demands. For I endorse and delight in the Law of God in my inmost self (with my new nature), But I discern in my bodily members (in my sensitive appetites and wills of the flesh) a different law (rule of action) at war against the law of my mind (my reason) and making me a prisoner to the law of sin that dwells in my bodily organs (in the sensitive appetites and wills of the flesh)". The question then is "Who will release and deliver me, from (the shackles of) this body of death?" Romans 7:25 triumphantly answers, "O thank God! (He will) through Jesus Christ (the Anointed One) our Lord! So then indeed I, of myself with the mind and heart, serve the Law of God, but with the flesh the law of sin". Therefore, live and "walk in the Spirit, and you shall not fulfil the lust of the flesh" (Galatians 5:16 NKJV).

This means that we do not continue with dual natures. Romans 6:1-6 clearly declares, "What shall we say then? Shall we continue in sin, that grace may abound? God forbid. How shall we that are dead to sin live any longer there? Know you not, that so many of us as were baptized into Jesus Christ were baptized into his death? Therefore we are buried with him by baptism into death: that like (just) as Christ was raised from the dead by the glory of the Father, even so we also should walk in newness of life. For if we have been planted together in the likeness of His death, we shall be also (be) in the likeness of His resurrection: Knowing this, that our old man (pre-conversion nature) is crucified with Him, that the body of sin might be destroyed, that henceforth we should not serve sin". We are now identified with Christ in His death (He died for the sins of this world), in burial (freed from sin) and resurrection (new life in the Spirit of God and of Christ, in the Holy Spirit). It is the Spirit that quickens. The Victory of Faith is Christ in us, His fullness so that there is no more room for the law of sin to operate; now it is Christ in us Our Hope of Glory (in this life and in the eternity to come when our redemption is complete).

Romans 8:10-16 tells it like it is, "And if (since) Christ be in you, the body (flesh) is dead because of sin; but the Spirit is life because of righteousness. But if (since) the Spirit of Him (God) that raised up Jesus from the dead dwell in you, He that raised up Chris from the dead shall also quicken (make alive)your mortal bodies by His Spirit that dwells in you. Therefore, brethren, we are debtors, not to the flesh, to live after the flesh. For if ye live after the flesh, ye shall die: but if ye through the spirit do mortify (make as dead) the deeds of the body (flesh), ye shall live. For as many as are led by the Spirit of God, they are the sons of God". He that is dead is freed from sin and alive unto God through Jesus Christ our Lord.

GOD'S LOVING PROVISION PREVAILS

God has given to us His Son as our gift of Love to cleanse us and redeem us and reconcile us back to Him. He has given to us His Spirit of Truth that is our comforter and guide, Christ in us the Hope of Glory. Jesus Christ the Lord, the Son of God became flesh and dwelt among us so that as the Son of man He was God's perfect (sinless and pure) sacrifice necessary to eradicate sin once and for all, permanently not only because God wanted His created beings made in His image to be pure and Holy as He and separated unto Himself, free from sin, but because also God will not allow sin to come into His presence. Habakkuk 1:13 reveals, "Thou (God) at of purer eyes than to behold evil, and canst not look on iniquity".

Christ died to take away, obliterate and completely destroy the sin in our lives. The wrath of God is ever an always against our sin. Disobedience and lawlessness against God and the sin within our hearts and minds and bodies are an abomination unto God. Hebrews 12:1 exhorts the children of God (of faith) to "lay aside (get rid of) every weight (anything that hinders us from serving God) and the sin that does so easily beset us (entraps us and deceives us into sinning against God) and run with patience the race (of life) that is set before us, Looking unto Jesus the author and finisher of our faith". We need to be washed in the blood of the lamb. God loves the sinner, but cannot tolerate the sin in our lives. Jesus blood was shed to cleanse us from sin; to forgive us our sins; to blot out our sin; to destroy the sin of the flesh thereby making us His new created beings by the cleansing blood of the lamb, Jesus.

Those who will not forsake their sin, or ask forgiveness of their sin, or come to Jesus that His blood may cleans them from all sin and impute unto them His righteousness; will be judged because of their sin. They stand condemned because they did not allow Jesus to forgive them, or cleanse them, and reconcile them back to God by His own blood shed at Calvary. Sin will be judged in the lives of sinners who will be pronounced guilty before the White Throne of God and sentenced for eternity to the place prepared for the Devil and his angels.

In the parable of the Wheat and the Tares Jesus said that the Kingdom of Heaven (on earth) is likened unto a man that sowed good seed in his field and while they slept his enemy came and sowed tares among the wheat(good seed). In the explanation Jesus said in Matthew 13:37-39, "He that soweth the good seed is the Son of man (Jesus Himself); The field is the world, the good seed are the children (son and daughters) of the kingdom(of God); but the tares are the children of the wicked one (Satan); The enemy that sowed them (tares, those who are not His disciples because they have rejected Jesus, God's Son and have embraced sin in their lives) is the devil; the harvest is the end of the world (age); and the reapers are the angels".

GOD'S LOVE FOUND IN HIS GRACE AND FAITH

God's Love is a never ending and ever extending process in the blessings that He continually bestows upon us. Psalm 103:1-5 reveals His loving kindness toward us, "Bless the Lord, O my soul: and all that is within We bless His Holy Name. Bless the Lord, O my soul, and forget not all His benefits: Who forgiveth all thine iniquities; Who healeth all thy diseases; Who redeemeth thy life from destruction; Who crowneth thee with loving-kindness and tender mercies; Who satisfieth thy mouth with good things; so that thy youth is renewed like the eagle's".

Ephesians 2:1-6 reveals that God's Love through His Grace and Faith, "And you hath He quickened (made alive), who were dead in trespasses and sins; Wherein in time past ye walked according to the course of this world, according to the prince of the power of the air, the spirit that now worketh in the children of disobedience. Among whom also we all had our conversation in times past in the lusts of our flesh, fulfilling the desires of the flesh and of the mind; and were by nature the children of wrath, even as others. But God, who is rich in mercy (loving kindness), for His great love wherewith He Loved us, Even when we were dead in sins, hath quickened (made alive)us together with Christ (by grace ye are saved); And hath raised us up together, and made us sit together in heavenly places in Christ Jesus".

In the Classical Greek language of the New Testament there are listed a number of ways this particular word for grace, charis is used. It may refer to God's free gift or benefit (Ephesians 2:8, "For by Grace are ye saved though faith; and that not of yourselves: it is the gift of God"); God's favor (Romans 12:6, "Having then gifts differing according to the grace that is given to us"); also joy, liberality, pleasure, and thanks worthy. After hours of studying about God's Grace and having experienced His Grace in my life I believe that God's Grace is God's compassionate mercy, freely and benevolently bestowed upon His created children as an outpouring of His great Love through Christ Jesus His Son. In essence God's Grace is experiential, God's Law of the Spirit of Life in Christ Jesus operating in our lives and freeing us from the Law of sin and death.

Romans 5:1-8 we find that because of God's so great love for us He made it possible for us to be justified (made righteous) by faith and receive free access into His Grace through the blood of Jesus Christ His Son. "Therefore, being justified by faith, we have peace with God through our Lord Jesus Christ: by Whom also we have access by faith into this grace wherein we stand, and rejoice in hope of the glory of God (God's abiding glorious presence). And not only so, but we glory in tribulations also: knowing that tribulation worketh patience (produces perseverance); And patience, (worketh) experience; and experience, hope: And hope maketh not ashamed (does not disappoint), because the love of God is shed abroad (poured out into) our hearts by the Holy Spirit which is given unto us. For when we were yet without strength, in due time (at God's appointed time) Christ died for the ungodly. For scarcely for a righteous man will one die: yet peradventure (perhaps) for a good man some would even dare to die. But God commended His love toward us, in that, while we were yet sinners, Christ died for us. Much more then, having been justified by His blood, we shall be saved from wrath through Him" (Jesus).

CHAPTER SIX

GOD'S LOVE MANIFESTED IN JESUS CHRIST HIS SON

THE GOSPEL MESSAGE OF JESUS, GOD'S GIFT OF LOVE

Matthew, Mark, Luke and John begin the New Testament (Covenant of Love as the four gospels or good news) message concerning Jesus the Christ the Son of God and the Son of man. Matthew, Mark and Luke are referred to as the synoptic Gospels because they give a synopsis (viewed together as one – a collective view) of the life of Jesus as He lovingly ministered unto the people. Each Gospel presents a different picture of Jesus life on earth. In Matthew Jesus is presented as a benevolent King (one who loves His people); in Mark Jesus is presented as the Perfect Servant (one who serves from a heart of love); in Luke Jesus is presented as the Son of man (one who loves His neighbor as himself). John, whose Gospel message is about the Deity of Jesus; the Christ, the Messiah (anointed one of God); the Creator of the world; the only begotten of the Father; The Lamb of God and The revelation of the great "I AM" (Exodus 3:14), presents Jesus as the Son of God.

The Love of God through Jesus His Son as the anointed Son of man is evident through the many parables that Jesus spoke to His people. The miracles and healings of Jesus also manifested God's love to us. Matthew 9:35-36 records, "And Jesus went about all the cities and villages, teaching in their synagogues, and preaching the gospel of the kingdom, and healing every sickness and every disease among the people. But (because) when he saw the multitudes, He was moved with compassion (loving kindness) on (for) them, because they fainted (were weary of the afflictions of life), and were scattered abroad, as sheep having no shepherd" (no one to love and care for them).

THE DEITY OF LOVE IN THE PERSON OF JESUS CHRIST THE SON OF GOD

The main theme of the Gospel of John is the Deity of Jesus Christ. His Deity is revealed in every

Chapter of the Gospel of John. In every revelation of His Deity Jesus reveals that God is Love and Jesus Christ ministry is a ministry of love. Everything that God does through His only begotten Son is for the benefit of His creation, mankind. Jesus speaks seven specific times concerning what He came to be to the people of His creative fiat. Jesus said, "I am the Bread of Life (John 6:35, our spiritual nourishment and sustenance); "I AM the Light of the world (John 8:12, the revelation of Truth concerning God's love for His creation); "Before Abraham was, I AM" (John 8:58, showing God's Love from eternity to eternity); "I AM the Good Shepherd" (John 10:11, revealing His compassionate love in that He cares for us); "I AM the resurrection, and the Life" (John 11:25, the promise of the Father in a resurrected life, of freedom from sin and its effects, of love, joy and peace and eternal life); "I AM the Way, the Truth, and the Life" (John 14:6, All things concerning the Father's love for us His created beings is revealed through Jesus Christ as the Way to God, the Truth concerning God, and our Life in God; "I AM the True Vine" (John 15;1, Jesus as the Son of man and the Son of God is the source of God's loving spiritual, emotional, mental and physical provision to His beloved children). Because God, " so loved the world, He gave to us His only begotten Son, what whosoever believeth in Him should not perish, but have everlasting life".

JESUS CHRIST – GOD'S ANOINTED SAVIOR

Christ is the Greek word for the anointed one and His anointing. It refers to the Messiah, God's promised gift of Love to His people that through Him they might be forgiven, cleansed from sin, reconciled back to God, filled with His Spirit, anointed, filled with all the blessings of God and welcomed by God into His Kingdom of Heaven as Heirs of Salvation and Sons and Daughters of His Love. Jesus is the living example and Divine pattern of life that God had from the beginning desired for every one of His created children. We are to be like Him, Jesus. Jesus reveals to us the kind of life that we are to live before our Father in Heaven. Jesus as the Son of man honored His Father and His Father said, "This is my beloved Son in Whom I am well pleased" (Matthew 3:37, Mark 1:11, Luke 3:22). Jesus reached out to the infirmed and compassionately healed the sick. Jesus eased the pain of the afflicted and destroyed the yoke of the oppressed. Jesus showed the Father's Love to His creation and came to show them the way (access) to the Father; to reveal to them the truth about how God so loved them that He sent Him (Jesus)that they may know the Father's will and purpose for their lives. Jesus demonstrated that we are to love our Father God with all our heart, with all our soul, with all our mind and strength; and to love our neighbor (fellowman) as our selves.

It is evident by the Word of God (see Romans chapters 6 and 7; James 1:13-15; I John 1:15-17) that without Jesus the Anointed Son of God as the Son of man and His Anointing of the Holy Spirit, man is not able to sustain the oppressive assaults of that wicked one, Satan. Satan is the arch-enemy of God and of His creation and by deceit and manipulation uses Gods precious crowning jewels of His creative fiat as dupes or pawns in his devious scheme to deceive and destroy and murder.

THE ANOINTING OF THE SPIRIT OF THE LORD GOD

Isaiah 61:1-2 proclaims God's prophetic message of salvation revealed to Zion by the Holy Spirit of Truth concerning the coming Messiah. It is the same message given in Luke 4:18 revealed as the anointing of the Holy Spirit. "The Spirit of the Lord is upon me, because He hath anointed Me to preach the gospel to the poor (in spirit), He hath sent Me to speak deliverance to the captives, and recovering of sight to the blind, to set at liberty them that are bruised, to peach the acceptable year of the Lord". Then what is The Anointing? Jesus is the Christ, the Messiah, and the Anointed One of God. The Holy Spirit Anointed Jesus the Son of God for His special assignment, here on earth among His created beings, as the Son of man. It is God's Holy Unction upon, a special favor or privilege for, those who gladly receive God's Gospel Message of Salvation. Jesus special assignment was to be the Messiah (Anointed Savior) by preaching God's Gospel Message of Truth: salvation to the uttermost for all who would believe and receive this special blessing of God. This included freedom from the galling fetters of sin; freedom of the oppressive works of the Devil; receiving the illuminating light of the Gospel that opens spiritual eyes to God's Truth of Love and redemption; healing us from all sicknesses and diseases and God's special benevolent blessings that He desires to lovingly bestow upon His children. Again, carefully, prayerfully and meditatively reread Luke

4:18 in the Amplified Bible, these prophetic words of Jesus, "The Spirit of the Lord (is) upon Me, because He has anointed Me (the Anointed One, the Messiah) to preach the good news (the Gospel) to the poor; He has sent Me to announce release to the captives and recovery of sight to the blind, to send forth as delivered those who are oppressed (who are downtrodden, bruised, crushed, and broken down by calamity)".

THE ANOINTING IS FOR OUR MISSION HERE ON EARTH

Jesus was anointed by the Holy Spirit of Truth for His special assignment given by God the Father as Messiah, Anointed Savior to the entire world. Those who receive Jesus and His message of Truth and Life and Light are anointed as Saints of God. The Greek word for Saint is hagios which has several interrelated meanings all of which reflect "if any man is in Christ he is a new creation, old things are passed away and behold all things are become new". It literally means to be separated from the common condition and mundane things of this world unto God. It is being in Christ and Christ in us. It is being crucified with Christ, yet alive in Him as Christ lives in us. It is being not conformed to this world but transformed by the renewing of our minds that we may prove that good and acceptable and perfect will of God. It is being sanctified, a status or place of continual cleansing from sin by the precious blood of Jesus, as we confess our sins He is faithful and just to forgive us our sins and cleanse us from all unrighteousness. It is a realization that we are not our own, with a price we have been bought (the precious blood of Jesus) and now as the Temple of the Holy Spirit we are to live a life that glorifies God in our body and in our spirit which now belong to God eternally. We now live a life of faith, believing God for without faith it is impossible to please God.

The Anointing endows us with everything that is necessary for God's Divine power to empower us to overcome Satan and the life destroying sin he deceitfully presents to mankind. The Anointing destroys all of the strongholds and imaginations of Satan's arsenal of evil. It is the yoke destroying, devil defeating, life resurrecting and most blessed assurance that Jesus is mine (personal tense) and I am His and share His triumphant victory over death, hell, sin and the grave. It is the Holy Spirit working, edifying and perfecting in us all that pertains to life and godliness. It is God's shield of truth, His feathers of comforting assurance and protection and His wings of Trust. The Anointing will enable the armor of the Lord to be effective in power of performance. The anointing, the wonder working power of the blood of Jesus is demonstratively operative in the lives of God's sons and daughters who are joint heirs with Jesus Christ in His Kingdom to come.

JESUS - GOD'S WORD OF LIGHT AND LOVE

The Gospel of John is a Gospel of Love beginning with God Who is Love through Jesus Christ His Son as His Gift of Love to all of mankind in the power of the Holy Spirit of Love. This Gospel clearly reveals Jesus is one with the Father and is not only His Son but His Word in all things. "In the beginning was the Word (Jesus) and the Word was with God, and the Word was God. The same was in the beginning with God. All things were made by Him; and without Him was not anything made that was made. In Him was the life, and the Life was the Light of men. And the Light sinneth in darkness, and the darkness comprehended it not (not able to comprehend or understand or grasp mentally or spiritually)" (John 1:5). The Word was God means that Jesus is one with the Father as the second person of the Holy Trinity or our Triune God. Therefore Jesus is God's Eternal Word of Love from the beginning. According to John 1:14 The Word became incarnate (flesh), "And the Word was made flesh, and dwelt among us (His creation), and we beheld His glory, the glory as of the only begotten of the Father,) full of grace and truth" (John 1:14).

Jesus as the Word is the voice of God spoken to mankind from the beginning. In creation when God said, "Let there be" it was Jesus Who was the word that spoke. All of the inspiration of the Old and New Testaments given through the Prophets and Apostles is from the Holy Spirit of Truth. This in essence is Jesus speaking because the Holy Spirit is the Spirit of Christ and of God and the Holy Spirit only speaks the Word of the Father through Jesus Christ the Son. He is called the Holy Spirit of Truth (John 14:17) because according to John 14:6, Jesus is the Truth. In John 14:24 and 26 Jesus says, "He that loves me not keeps not my sayings (words) and the word which ye hear is not mine, but the Father's which sent me". And in verse 26, "But the Comforter, which is the Holy Ghost, Whom the Father will send in My name (Jesus), He shall teach you all things, and bring all things to your remembrance whatsoever I (Jesus) have said unto you" (the anointing).

I John 2:8-9 reveal Jesus as the light of love, "Again a new commandment (God's illuminating Word of Love)I write unto you, which thing is true in Him (Jesus) and in you (children of God); because the darkness is past and the true light now shineth. He that saith he is in the light (concerning the love of Jesus) and hates his brother is in darkness even until now. He that loves his brother abideth in the light, and there is non-occasion of stumbling in him". John 5:39 exhorts us to search (study and mediate) upon the Word of God, rightfully dividing (interpreting) its message of Love. "Search (actually a command of God to us, you search) the scriptures; for in them you think you have eternal life and they are they which testify of Me". In II Timothy 2:15 Jesus the Word of Truth exhorts us to , "Study to show thyself approved unto God, a workman (disciple of Jesus Christ doing the work of God in the anointing) that needeth not to be ashamed, rightly dividing the Word of Truth". Again, In II Timothy 3:16 God reveals to us ,"All Scripture (His Holy Word) is given by inspiration of God (through the anointing of the Holy Spirit of Truth), and is profitable (God's superior favor and empowerment) for doctrine (God's truth for instruction in life), for reproof (it convicts of the error of sin-to rebuke wrong thinking), for correction (to give God's position of what is Right), for instruction (God the Father teaching His children what is Right) in righteousness (justified in the presence of God): That the man of God may be perfect (mature in Christ), thoroughly furnished (to be provided with His Righteousness) unto all good works".

When John 1:4 reveals that Jesus is the life that was the Light of men He was revealing to us not only the illuminating power of God's Light for revelation of His Truth (Jesus as the Word and as the Revelation and the Life) but also God's purifying Light that purges (cleanses us from the roots up) from all sin. It is in and through Jesus the Light (illuminating power) of the Word whereby we can become pure before our Holy God (John 8:12). It is a Light that overcomes death, "I Am the resurrection, and the life; he that believeth in Me, though he were dead (may die), yet shall he live" (John 11:125). Therefore, Jesus as the Light is God's pathway of life for righteous living and Jesus is the Truth (revelation of what is Right) and Jesus as the life is our example of a life that is pleasing to God, (John 14:6).

JESUS THE SON OF MAN – GOD'S WORD OF LOVE PERSONIFIED

It is my earnest prayer and fervent desire that I adequately explain the essence of God's love revealed by His Holy Spirit because the Holy Spirit searches the deep things of God especially the love of God. The first fruit of the Spirit (Galatians 5:22) is love because love is the essence that identifies all of the fruit. God through Paul's prayer recorded in Ephesians 3:18-19 affirmed His desire, "That Christ may dwell in your hearts by faith; that ye, being rooted and grounded in love, May be able to comprehend (fully understand) with all saints what is the breadth, and length, and depth, and height; And to know the love of Christ, which passeth knowledge, that ye might be filled with all the fullness of God". It is a matter of the heart (Spirit of Truth in our spirit) not of the human intellect or finite mind of man.

I Corinthians 2:9-1 reveals, "Eye has not seen, nor ear heard, neither have entered into the heart of man, the things which God hath prepared for them that love Him. But God hath revealed them unto us by His Spirit: for the Spirit searches all things, yea the deep things of God". Romans 8:27 further states, "And He that searches the hearts knoweth what is the mind of the Spirit, because He maketh intercession for the saints according to the will of God". We are therefore to love God with our entire being: heart (spirit), soul (emotions), mind (intellect) and body. Since God is Love, when He breathed into man His breath of life He imparted to man His ability to love even as God so loved us. God has given to us faith (that operates by love) or the ability to believe Him unquestioningly and without reservation.

It is impossible for God's created human race to love with the agape (God kind of love) without first receiving within their (our) spirit God's Gift of Love, "Christ in you the Hope of Glory" (Colossians 1:27). Jesus came down from His Throne in Glory to become the Son of man that He may demonstrate that God truly so loved His created beings that He gave His most precious gift of love, Jesus Christ His Son. The only answer to such a divine sacrificial act of God is His love. The Supreme Judge of the universe (which He created) utilized all of His Divine attributes in creating and sustaining His sons and daughters for all eternity. In fact The Living Word of God is His love letter to us, His beloved creation. He has filled us with His divine power and promise of life and godliness that can never be broken because it has been declared by Almighty God Himself. It is fulfilled in the person of His Word, Jesus, His only begotten Son and our Faithful Witness in the power of the Holy Spirit of Truth. These proverbial words of Solomon under the inspiration of the Spirit of God said, "I love them that love me, and those that seek me early (diligently) shall find me. Riches and honor are with me; yea, durable (enduring) riches and righteousness. My fruit is better than gold, yea, than fine gold; and my revenue than choice silver. I lead in the way of righteousness, in the midst of the paths of judgment: That I may cause those that love me to inherit substance (wealth); and I will fill their treasures" (Proverbs 8:17-21).

JESUS THE SON OF MAN IS GOD'S ETERNAL WORD OF TRUTH

Hebrews 13:8 reveals that, "Jesus Christ (is) the same yesterday, today and forever. In Malachi 3:6 God (Jesus) says, "I Am the Lord, I change not". Peter declares in Acts 2:36, "that God hath made that same Jesus, whom ye have crucified, both Lord and Christ". Since Jesus is the Word of God and is equal with God as the second person of the Holy Trinity, it is His affirmation also. There is no disagreement or shadow of difference of what is truth and righteousness between the members of the Holy Trinity of Father, Son and Holy Spirit. They are One. Paul wrote in Ephesians 4:4-6, "There is one body, and one Spirit, even as ye are called in one hope of your calling; One Lord, one faith, one baptism (of the Holy Spirit), One God and Father of all, Who is above all, and through all, and in you all". John 14 reveals to us that God's bond of perfectness, Agape Love is manifested as God the Father being in Christ and Christ in the Father God and together they abide in His redeemed sons and daughters of faith in the person of the Holy Spirit within our spirit. Read John chapters 14 through 17 and let the Holy Spirit reveal to your heart the glorious truth of His Word in our relationship with the Holy Trinity of Father, Son and Holy Spirit.

In creation when God spoke (through Jesus His Word of Truth) He said, "Let there be" and there was! There is no difference in the power of

Jesus as the Word in creation, in salvation, in healing, in righteousness, in provision, in anything or anywhere that God's Word of Power manifests itself. Jesus said to the paralytic of Matthew 9:2-7, "Son, be of good cheer, thy sins be forgiven thee" and to "take up thy bed and walk". Jesus was revealing His power as the Word of God in all things that pertain to life and godliness. In verse 5 & 6 Jesus says to the religious multitude, "For which is easier to say, 'Your sins be forgiven you'; or to say, 'Arise, and walk'? But that ye may know that the Son of man hath power on earth to forgive sins, (then saith He (Jesus) to the sick of the palsy,) "Arise, take up they bed, and go unto your house".

It is important that we know and understand God through His Word and Spirit of Truth. Although the Word of God plainly reveals that without God's revelation all that pertains to God as Father and Jesus as the Son and the Holy Spirit of Truth is a mystery, yet in Christ God's Word of Truth is a revelation, unveiling, baring so that all things are open and naked. Hebrews 4:12-13 reveals, "For the Word of God is quick (alive), and powerful, and sharper (cuts keenly and precisely) than any twoedged sword, piercing even to the dividing asunder of soul and spirit (of man), and of the joints and marrow, and is a discerner of the thoughts and intents of the heart. Neither is there any creature that is not manifest (hidden from) in His sight; but all things are naked and opened (revealed) unto the eyes of Him (God) with Whom we have to do" (must give an account to or be judged by).

THE MYSTERY OF THE WORD OF GOD REVEALED

In my previous writing, "Behold I Show You a Mystery" I endeavored under the inspiration of the Holy Spirit to reveal that God's Word is in essence a revelation of the mysteries of the Word of God, but that it is only accessed by those who desire to know about God in all of His essence: Father, Son and Holy Spirit. Throughout His New Covenant with His new creation in Christ Jesus, God reveals Himself; His mystery of His Kingdom; His Will; His beloved Son Jesus Christ as Messiah; His Gospel Message (God's Good News to man); His hidden truths of the ages concerning His creation and generations of His saints; the riches of His Glory; of iniquity (lawlessness-sin); of faith; and of Godliness. The final Chapter (Book of Revelation) of the Word of God contains the mystery of eternity beginning with the Revelation (Jesus the Christ, the Son of God as the Son of man) and the panoramic view of the final days of earth as we know it, a brief overview of the Church Age, the Rapture, the Tribulation Period, the New Heaven and the New (renovated-made new) earth.

God's revelation of truth is His volition of His so great love for His creation, those made in His image. This revelation of Love is made manifest so that we might "know Him and the power of His resurrection, and the fellowship of His sufferings, being made conformable unto His death" (Philippians 3:10). The mystery of such love that God has poured out upon His created beings is found throughout the New Testament and reveals that God wanted us His creation to know about His so great love for us. That God would love us even while we were yet sinners and had rejected Him. That God wanted to open His gates of heaven and live and fellowship with those who caused His suffering and pain and death upon Calvary. That God would redeem a worthless slave of Satan and sin who defied God's love and grace. That God would take me as I am, love me as His own, forgive me of all my sin, clothe me in His robes of righteousness and seat me with Him in heavenly places and make me a joint heir with His Son Jesus. That God would open wide His arms of grace and draw me into His arms of love divine that ransomed me. Truly, who can know such love? Everyone whom God has created is included in God's invitation of Love, "Come unto me all ye who labor and are heavy laden and I will give you rest".

THE MYSTERY OF GOD'S LOVE REVEALED

Mark 4:11 Jesus had just taught His disciples and the people the Truth of the Kingdom of God through the parable of the Sower saying to His disciples, "Unto you it is given to know the mystery of the kingdom of God: but unto them that are without (who do not know about the things of God), all these things are done in parables".

Romans 11:25 reveals the mystery of the restoration of Israel as a nation which we saw happen in 1948, "For I would not, brethren, that ye should be ignorant of this mystery, lest ye should be wise in your own conceits; that blindness in part is happened to Israel until the fullness of the

Gentiles come in".

Romans 16:25-26 reveals one of the prophetic mysteries concerning Jesus Christ, "Now to Him (Jesus) that has the power to establish you according to My Gospel, and the preaching of Jesus Christ, according to revelation of the mystery, which was kept secret since the world began, But now is made manifest and by the scriptures of the prophets, according to the commandment of the everlasting God, made known to all nations for the obedience of faith".

I Corinthians 2:4-7 speaks of the mystery of the Wisdom of God in a world beset with the wisdom of finite man, "And my speech and my preaching was not with enticing words of man's wisdom, but in demonstration of the Spirit and of power: That your faith should not stand in the wisdom of men, but in the power of God. Howbeit we speak wisdom among them that are perfect (mature) yet not the wisdom of this world, nor of the princes of this world; that come to nought: But we speak of the wisdom of God in a mystery, even the hidden wisdom, which God ordained before the world (God had planned before creation) unto our glory".

At the beginning of the Word of God to the Ephesians Paul wrote about the love of God revealed in His bountiful spiritual blessings in Christ. Then beginning with verse 9 through 11 Paul writes, "Having made known unto us the mystery of His will, according to His good pleasure, which He hath purposed in Himself: That in the dispensation of the fullness of time He might gather together in one (Jew and Gentile) all things in Christ, both which are in heaven, and which are on earth; even in Him".

At the beginning of Ephesians 3 Paul reveals his mission given to him in person by Jesus Christ, to preach the Gospel of Christ and the dispensation of the Grace of God to the gentiles, "How that by revelation; He (Jesus) made known unto me the mystery; (as I wrote afore in few words. Whereby, when ye read, ye may understand my knowledge in the mystery of Christ) Which in other ages was not made known unto the sons of men, as it is now revealed unto His holy apostles and prophets by the Spirit; That the Gentiles should be fellow heirs, and of the same body and partakers of His promise in Christ by the Gospel" (Ephesians 3:3-6).

In Ephesians 5:22-33 Paul writes symbolically about the Church in terms of the relationship of husband and wife. We are to love our wife even as Christ loves us, the Church. Jesus (as the Son of man) sanctified the Church with His own blood and the washing of the Word, "that He might present it to Himself (Our resurrected King of Kings and Lord of Lords) a glorious Church, not having spot (blemish) or wrinkle (distorting influence), or any other such thing; but that it should be holy (separated unto Him even as a husband and wife become one flesh) and without blemish". Then Paul concludes that, "This is a great mystery, but I speak concerning Christ and the Church" (Ephesians 5:32).

Paul's burning desire was that he would be able to preach the Gospel Message of Jesus Christ crucified buried and resurrected in simple truth that God's plan of redemption would be made known to them. "And for me, that utterance may be given unto me, that I may open my mouth, boldly, to make known the mystery of the Gospel" (Ephesians 6:19) Again in Colossians 1:25-26 Paul writes, "Whereof I am made a minister, according to the dispensation of God which is given to me for you, to fulfill the Word of God; Even the mystery which hath been hid from ages and from generations, but now is made manifest to his saints: To Whom God would make known what is the riches of the glory of the mystery among gentiles, which is Christ in you, the hope of glory".

Paul in Colossians 2:2-3 reveals the love of God in opening their blind eyes to the truth of God the Father, God the Son and God the Holy Spirit, "That their hearts might be comforted, being knit together in love, and unto all riches of the full assurance of understanding, to the acknowledgement of the mystery of God, and of the Father, and of Christ (His Messiah); In Whom are hid all the treasures of wisdom and knowledge".

The love of God is demonstrated in the life, death and resurrection of His Son Jesus as the Son of man, the Christ, our Messiah and living Lord. Colossians 4:3 states, "Withal praying also for us, that God would open unto us (Paul and his missionary co-laborers) a door of utterance, to speak the mystery of Christ, for which I am also in bonds". Paul said in Romans 1:16, "For I am not ashamed of the Gospel of Christ: for it is the power of God unto salvation to everyone that believeth; to the Jew first and also the Greek (gentile)".

Even in man's rebellion against God and all that He has provided for them God's love for His created beings has not diminished. He does not want mankind to be in spiritual darkness and therefore He has revealed through His Word the true character and intent of iniquity (lawless behavior against Almighty God). II Thessalonians 2:7-10 states, "For the mystery of iniquity doth already work: only He (Holy Spirit) Who now letteth (restrains-holds back the forces of evil) will let until he (Satan) is taken out of the way. And then that Wicked (wicked one-Satan) be revealed, whom the Lord shall consume with the spirit (breath) of his mouth, and shall destroy with the brightness of his coming: Even him (the anti-Christ of the last days) whose coming is after the working of Satan with all (evil) power and signs and lying wonders, And with all deceivableness of unrighteousness in them that perish; because they received not the love of the Truth, that they might be saved". Jesus, Christ in us has made us to be the "salt of the earth" that we may be ambassadors of Christ in this world of sin and be a preserving and purifying agent (our spirit in the power of the Holy Spirit) of salvation for those dead in trespasses and sins (Matthew 5:13).

God's love is also demonstrated through the faith of His chosen leaders who hold (possess) the, "mystery of the faith in a pure conscience" (I Timothy 3:9). God has revealed His love to us in everything that He has planned, ordained, spoken, acted upon, created, provided, purified, sanctified, prepared, revealed and judged and especially in every way that He has revealed Himself as the Almighty God, the I AM that I AM.

God has given to us His manual of love, the Holy Bible, the Word of God that from "In the beginning" through to the last Amen He might reveal to us the mystery of Godliness. "And without controversy great is the mystery of Godliness: God was manifest in the flesh (Christ in us the Hope of Glory, justified (made righteous) in the Spirit, seen of angels, preached unto the Gentiles, believed on in this world, received up into glory".

The Revelation of God's gift of love to mankind, Jesus, is written by none other than the disciple whom Jesus so loved, John the Apostle. It clearly reveals the things which John saw through the vision given to Him of Christ as the Alpha and Omega, the beginning and the end of all things, including our faith; the things which are (the Church dispensation);

the things which shall be hereafter (the rapture, fulfillment of the redemption of the Church); the Tribulation period and the New Heaven and the New Earth in the millennial Kingdom of our Lord and Savior, Jesus Christ the Son of God.

CHAPTER SEVEN

GOD'S LOVE MANIFESTED IN OUR SALVATION

JESUS IS MESSIAH (SAVIOR)

From the beginning, before the foundations of the world were laid, before God's creative fiat God had appointed Jesus and Jesus willingly accepted His title and position as Messiah. In the Hebrew of the Old Testament it is Mashiyach and is interpreted as the anointed, consecrated, sanctified Son of God. The prophetic commandment of God to restore and rebuild the Temple after the Hebrew children's captivity in Babylon began the 40 year period of 70 weeks (a week equaling 7 years) of Daniel 9:25-26. "Know therefore and understand, that from the going forth of the commandment to restore and build Jerusalem (Cyrus's decree) unto the Messiah the Prince (Jesus) shall be seven weeks, and threescore and two weeks (483 years): the street (open square of Jerusalem) shall be built again, and the wall (moat), even in troublous times" (the opposition by Sanballat, Tobiah, Arabians, Ammonites and the Ashdodies). Then in verse 26, "And after threescore and two weeks shall Messiah be cut off" (Jesus crucified). In the Greek language of the New Testament it is Messias or Mashiyach: the Messias or Christ. In John 1:41 Andrew says, "We have found the Messiah" (Mashiyach which is, being interpreted or translated Christ, the Anointed One). Then the Samaritan woman at the well said to Jesus, "I know that Messiah (Messias) cometh, which is called Christ" (Christos).

Throughout the Word of God, His timetable for all events and situations and happenings in the world are right on time, no deviation. God is as exact and perfect in His creative fiat as He is in everything that He does. So when God said, "I so loved the world that I gave My only begotten Son that whosoever believeth in Him shall not perish but have everlasting life". You better believe it! When the Word says, "Whosoever believeth and liveth in Jesus the Christ shall be saved". You better believe it! When Jesus said, "the soul that sins, it shall die". You better believe it! God's word never returns to Him void but always accomplishes it purpose and God has no idle words to say. His Word is Truth and His Word is life.

The world system with its formidable intelligentsia that rejects the Word of God as myth and the intelligent design of the Universe, including the creation of man by God as a fable; is under the domination of Satan, the father of all lies. Those who follow them in complete trust is like the blind leading the blind and those who are following the blind and both fall in the ditch (pit) of oblivion or the Abyss of Hell. The reason for man's dilemma is his insatiable avarice, lust and egotism in promoting self above all others, including God. The world hates Christians because they hate, Jesus the Son of man as the Christ of God. They say, "No God or me", and in their determined attempts to justify their actions, they dig deeper their own grave of frustration, futility and finally death.

JESUS, GOD'S LOVE MANIFESTED IN OUR SALVATION

Jesus means Yahweh is Salvation. The angel said unto Mary, "You shall call His Name Jesus" for He is Christ (Messiah-Savior) and He shall save His people from all sin. His people are those who were predestined before the beginning of God's creative fiat. Those who were predestined are those who have received Jesus, the Son of man as God's Son and His sacrifice, the shedding of His own blood. God decreed from the beginning that only the blood of Jesus would be the acceptable sacrifice to cleanse us from sin and reinstate, restore, reconciles us back into a right relationship with God. Only Love would do this. Even the weapons of our warfare here on earth are of the Spirit of God and Love is our principle defense, our refuge, our fortress. No one, no power, no force, no demon of hell, nothing shall be able to separate us from the Love of God in Christ Jesus our Lord. Romans 8:35-39 emphatically proclaims, "Who shall separate us from the Love of Christ? Shall tribulation, or distress, or persecution, or famine, or nakedness, or peril, or sword? As it is written, For Your sake we are killed all the day long; we are accounted as sheep for the slaughter. No! In all these things we are more than conquerors through Him that loved us. For I am persuaded, that neither death, nor life, nor angels, nor principalities, nor powers, nor things present, nor things to come, nor height, nor depth, nor any other creature, shall be able to separate us from the Love of God which is in

Christ Jesus our Lord".

God has given our Savior the preeminence of power over all things in this world through His Salvation to whosoever will come. He is our Saviour, our Redeemer, our Protector, our Strength, our Deliverer, our Sustenance or Supplier of our every need, our Strong Tower, our Refuge, our High Priest and Mediator between man and God, our Justifier, our Judge, our Righteousness, our Sacrifice, our Faith, our Resurrected Lord and our All in All.

Now, let me speak to you about this Jesus. When I was a young man of eighteen I came into the Nazarene Church in South Bend, Indiana not knowing what to expect being a former member of another denomination. The message of the cross preached by the pastor was foreign to me as I did not know about salvation or what it entailed. I was nervous at first but after several weekly Sunday and Wednesday night visits I became aware of my predicament. Here was I, a young man just out of high school and living at the YMCA, working at Bendix Automotive and Aviation with few friends in the area. This Jesus the pastor spoke of said He loved me. One Sunday night during the message I felt in my spirit being that Jesus was tenderly inviting me to open my heart to His offer of Salvation. My heart yearned to know this Jesus, but I did not know how to approach Him. Then the pastor at the close of his message about the cross and blood of Jesus shed for me, gave an invitation to come to the altar and receive Jesus as Savior and Lord of my life. I finally yielded to the tender urging of the Holy Spirit and found my way down the aisle and to the altar where I wept and confessed my sins (they were many) and received Jesus sacrifice for me, as my redeemer. Many of the church members joined me at the altar and prayed for me. Suddenly, I felt this sweet peace come over my soul and at that point in time, I knew that Jesus loved me and received me and forgave me of all my sins and filled me with Himself.

GOD'S LOVE MANIFESTED IN THE CROSS OF CALVARY

The roughhewn cross of the Roman Empire is the most cruel, horrible, detestable, instrument of human torture and hate: the punishment by death that this world has ever known. Yet, the cross upon which Jesus died, stained with the precious blood of Jesus, the Son of God as the Son of man it has become a cross of love and glory. It caused Paul to cry out, "Forbid it Lord that I should glory, save in the cross of our Lord Jesus Christ, by Whom the world is crucified unto me, and I unto the world" (Galatians 6:14). The cross of Jesus throughout the ages of time since that day when Jesus died has become for millions a symbol of the Glory of Jesus Christ our Lord.

This same Jesus has been loving generations of people from that day He said; "It is finished" signifying that God's Love is established for eternity, accomplishing its purpose here on earth for all mankind: God's plan of salvation to the uttermost for everyone who believed and received His Son as Lord and Saviour. Even today, God's love is the same as it was in the beginning and as it will be throughout eternity. There is no sin that is unpardonable (except that sin against the Holy Spirit) if you will come to Jesus and ask Him to come into your life and be your Lord and Saviour. If you will obey the invitation of the Holy Spirit to come to Jesus and receive Him, you will be forgiven of all your sins, cleansed and washed in the blood of the lamb of God, Jesus, and filled with the Holy Spirit as an earnest (the love tie of assurance that binds you to Jesus), guarantee that you have been saved.

Oh, Love so amazing, so rich and pure truly exacts my soul, my life and my all. It is so important that you return God's love by receiving Jesus His Son as Lord and Savior of your life and live for Him Who died for you: your Eternal destination depends upon it. It is truly the only life worth the living. It is in fact, the life God planned for you even before you were even born. You were predestined to be a part of His family through Jesus Christ the Lord.

When Jesus died on the cross, His heart was pierced and opened up by a Roman spear and at that time God's heart was also opened to whosoever will come to Him through the blood of Jesus. It became the world's fountain of life and the beginning of mercy and grace for all who would plunge in and be covered by His blood and sacrifice of love.

CHAPTER EIGHT

GOD'S LOVE MANIFESTED IN HIS FAITH

JESUS THE AUTHOR AND FINISHER OF OUR FAITH

Hebrews 12:2 states that those who have Jesus as Lord and Savior are, "Looking unto Jesus the author and finisher of our faith; who for the joy that was set before Him endured the cross, despising the shame and is set down at the right hand of the throne of God". Our faith begins in Jesus and ends with Jesus in glory. For then we shall see Him as He is, face to face in all of His glory; when our faith has become sight.

Galatians 5:6 states, "For in Jesus Christ neither circumcision availeth anything, nor uncircumcision, but faith which worketh by Love". The Amplified Bible reads, "For (if we are) in Christ Jesus, neither circumcision nor uncircumcision counts for anything, but only faith activated and energized and expressed and working in love". The Greek word for Love used in this portion of scripture is Agape, the God kind of Love. Our measure of faith is from God. Divine Faith is man's response to God Who so loves His creation that in Love he gave to man the ability to accept God's Love: faith. Galatians 5:20 affirms, "I am crucified with Christ: nevertheless I live; yet not I, but Christ lives in me: and the life which I now live in the flesh I live by the faith of the Son of God, Who loved me, and gave Himself for me".

Love and faith go hand in hand as I Corinthians says that, "And now abides (dwells within the spirit and soul of man) faith, hope, charity (Agape – the God kind of love), these three; but the greatest of these is charity" (love). God's love for His creation, mankind excels all other loves that abide within His heart. The Psalmist David said, "What is man that you are mindful (so lovingly aware of) him? And the son of man, that you visit (fondly look after) him? For you have made him a little lower than the angels (Elohiym-Triune God), and have crowned (anointed) him with glory and honor. You made him to have dominion over the works of your hands (creation); (and) You have put all things under his feet" (Psalm 8). The most heaven sent revelation of God's Love for us is that familiar Word of God found in John 3:16, "For God so (in the nth degree of His Love) loved the world, that He gave His only begotten Son, that whosoever believeth in Him should not perish, but have everlasting life".

This verse of scripture becomes even more powerful when you realize that Jesus, the Son of God came to suffer, bleed and die in our behalf as the Son of man; to be sacrificed for all of humanity that we may have eternal life with Him as His eternal family. Jesus, Deity in the flesh, the only begotten Son of God in eternity before creation came to raise up unto God a family of sons and daughters who are like and in Him. To bring you and I and whosoever will in to a righteous relationship with God as His only begotten (Greek monogenes) of the Father in this world. Jesus as the only begotten of God describes the unique relationship of oneness of Jesus with His Father God. It distinguishes Jesus, the only Son of God (equal with God in eternity – the second person of the Holy Trinity) in contrast to God's children. Jesus came to glorify God through his suffering, shed blood and death upon Calvary (His crucifixion) by fulfilling God's prophetic promise that those predestined to become the sons and daughters of God would be God's only children.

Romans 10:9-13 reveals the simplicity of receiving God's full and free salvation through Jesus Christ His Son. "That if you shall confess with your mouth the Lord Jesus, and shall believe in your heart that God has raised Him from the dead, you shall be saved. For with the heart man believes unto righteousness; and with the mouth confession is made unto salvation. For the scripture says (plainly) whosoever believes on Him (Jesus) shall not be ashamed (put to shame). For there is no difference between the Jew and the Greek (gentile): for the same Lord over all is rich unto all that call upon Him. For, whosoever shall call upon the name of the Lord (Jesus) shall be saved."

CHAPTER NINE

GOD'S LOVE AND THE HOLY SPIRIT OF TRUTH

CHRIST IN YOU THE HOPE OF GLORY

John 14:15-26 reveals that the Love of God manifests itself within us (our spirit) through His Holy Spirit because He wants us to receive the victory from the battles He fought for us, especially that which was fought and won by Jesus on Calvary's Hill. In John 14:15-21 Jesus speaks of the promise of the Holy Spirit, "If you love me, keep My commandments. And I will pray (ask) the Father, and He shall give (to) you another Comforter (Christ in you) that He may abide with you forever. Even the Spirit of Truth, Whom the world cannot receive, because, it cannot see Him or (even) know Him; but you know Him, for He dwells within you". The Holy Spirit only dwells within the hearts (spirit) of the sons and daughters of God. In verse eighteen Jesus speaks again, "I will not leave you comfortless (without my presence): I will come unto you. Yet a little while, and the world will see me no more; but you will see me: because I live you shall live also. In that day (the day the Holy Spirit indwells you) you will know that I am (also) in my Father, and you in Me, and I in you (the presence of the Holy Spirit). He that has my commandments, and keeps them (within his spirit as the source of light and life), He is the one who truly loves me; and he that loves me shall be loved of (by) my Father, and I will love him, and will manifest (reveal) Myself to him".

In John 14:23 & 26 Jesus again speaks to us of His and His Father's love for us, "If a man love Me, he will keep My words: and My Father will love him and we will come unto him, and make our abode (home) with him" "But the Comforter, which is the Holy Ghost, Whom the Father will send in My name, He shall teach you all things, and bring all things to your remembrance, whatsoever I have said unto you". Jesus spoke always of the Father; His will, His purpose, and His Love. Therefore, the Holy Spirit will teach us about the love of God the Father though His beloved Son, Jesus Christ. The Holy Spirit teaches us how to love even as the Father manifests and demonstrates His love for us. The Word gives to us our pathway or walk of love in this life. It is also a picture of God's love for us. God's love is not as the world loves. God's love is unfeigned (not a pretense-but real) for God so loved us that He gave His most precious gift of love, Jesus to become our Savior. Although God is omnipotent and omniscient and omnipresent; and although God knows all things in His created universe; yet His love is the primary power or most fervent force of His Nature. His Holiness is manifested in His love, and the object of His love is His beloved creation, you and I. His love as lovingkindness suffers long and is not easily provoked. While we were yet sinners, Christ died for us. When God looked down from heaven and saw mankind's total disrespect for Him, He had and will continue to always have one thought in mind (to be mindful of) His created beings and bring them into His family of love. His love for us never fails for he always endeavors through Jesus Christ His Son, through His Word, and through His Holy Spirit of Truth, to bring us into His green pastures and beside His still waters and lead us in the paths of His righteousness. He has prepared and spread out before us for all to see that He has anointed us with His blessings of life; and that our cup truly runs over with the goodness of God; and that His mercy is with us wherever we may go in this world as His Son or daughter of light and the confidence that we have in Him is our assurance of eternal life.

It is evident from the Word of God that the Holy Spirit is the Spirit of God the Father and of God the Son and as such is God the Holy Spirit. All three that are the blessed Triune Godhead, agree in their work of love for their beloved creation of mankind. God the Father in His great love for us planned it all; Jesus the Son of God as the Son of man through His blood, death and resurrection fulfilled (finished) it all for us; and the Holy Spirit of Truth applies it to our hearts by faith and enables us to receive it all in the name of Jesus.

CHAPTER TEN

GOD'S LOVE MANIFESTED IN THE GIFTS OF THE HOLY SPIRIT

THE HOLY SPIRIT'S GIFT OF GRACE

"For by grace you have been saved through faith; and that not of yourselves: it is the gift of God: Not of works lest any man should boast. For we are His workmanship, created in Christ Jesus for good works, which God has before (the foundations of the world were laid) that we should walk in them". We have already touched on the meaning and fulfillment of God's Grace bestowed upon us, however let us reiterate the truth of its manifestation in our lives. The Holy Spirit is Christ in us our hope of Glory. The Holy Spirit administers in us all of the benefits of God in Christ Jesus through us. When Christ died upon the Cross, we as believers were baptized into Jesus (literally into His death) Romans 6:3. The finished work of Christ Jesus our Lord is, Christ in us the hope of glory. We are then in Christ (identified with His Finished Work on Calvary). We are His workmanship means that we are energized and anointed by the Holy Spirit to perform the works of God, until Jesus returns at the end of the age and receives us unto Himself that where He is we shall be also. This is when our redemption is fully realized and consummated. But until then, we have His Holy Spirit in us Who works in us the finished work of Christ on the Cross, "It is finished".

THE HOLY SPIRIT'S GIFT OF REVELATION

In John 14:17 Jesus refers to the Holy Spirit as the Spirit of Truth because He is the Spirit of Jesus, Who is the Truth and because He will reveal all things unto us. John 14:26 records these words of Jesus, "But, the Comforter, which is the Holy Ghost (Spirit), Whom the Father will send in My name, He shall teach you (reveal to you) all things, and bring all things to your remembrance, whatever I have said junto you." I Corinthians 1:9-10 further states, "But as it is written, 'Eye has not seen, nor ear heard, neither have entered into the heart of man, the things which God has prepared for them that Love Him'. But God has revealed them unto us by His Spirit: For the Spirit (Holy Spirit) searches all things, yea, the deep (hidden or mysteries) things of God." Therefore, "we speak the wisdom of God in a mystery, even the hidden wisdom, which God ordained (predetermined) before the world (ages) unto our glory" That is how much God loves us from before the worlds were made (creation); in His creative fiat (when He formed us and breathed into our form His gift of life); in Christ Jesus and His finished work on the Cross; in Jesus Resurrection; in our Anointing by Jesus through His finished work; and by His presence within us manifested by the Holy Spirit of Truth.

THE HOLY SPIRIT'S GIFT OF TONGUES

This has, because of Satan's influence, a point of disagreement within the body of Christ, because some have not sought God's purpose and will in speaking in tongues, the heavenly language of the Holy Spirit. I don't know why, but I can only tell you what I have experienced. I was initially against the gift of tongues, not knowing what it was, what part it had in my Christian life and whether or not it was really necessary, like the washing of the disciple's feet by Jesus. I too have been in feet washing ceremonies and through this experience I have received a blessing of fellowship and communion with my brother and sisters in Christ that was truly edifying.

Then, one day as I was reading the Word of God in I Corinthians 12:1-11 that spiritual gifts were given by the Holy Spirit, "concerning spiritual gifts brethren, I would not have you ignorant" (unknowing). God wanted to reveal these gifts to us and one of them was the gift of "divers (different) kinds of tongues and the interpretation of tongues ... dividing to every man severally (individually) as He (Holy Spirit) will" (I Corinthians 12:10-11). As I prayed and pondered on this passage of scripture, the Holy Spirit ministered unto me that on the day of Pentecost, diversity of tongues were given and interpreted so that the glorious truth of Salvation could be made known to all who had come to Jerusalem on Pentecost Sunday. Also, the Holy Spirit revealed unto me that it is the language of the Holy Spirit for each brother or sister in Christ, individually to speak those deep truths in our behalf to God: when with groaning's and fervency of my spirit I could not fully express.

Romans 8:26 states that, "Likewise the Spirit also helps our infirmities (weaknesses-inability in our own strength): for we know not what we should pray for as we ought: but the Spirit (Holy Spirit) Itself makes intercession (between us and God) for us with groaning's which cannot be uttered. And He (the Holy Spirit) that searches the hearts (of men) knoweth; what is the mind of the Spirit, because He makes intercession for the saints according to the will of God".

There is no doubt about it. According to the Word of God and the Holy Spirit of Truth, speaking in tongues is our willingness to let the Holy Spirit speak in and through us the deep things of God, the things that the Holy Spirit of God knows we want to say, but because the flesh clouds our minds and the petition, we need the help of the Holy Spirit. Jesus even prays for us per John 17:9, 15, 20, "I pray for them: I pray not for the world, but for them which you have given me (by the Holy Spirit through the Cross of Jesus); for they are yours" and "I pray not that You (God His Father) should take them out of the world, but that You should keep them from the evil one" and "Neither pray I for them alone, but for them also that shall believe on Me through their word".

When I asked the Lord for direction, we (Joanne my wife and I) were invited to go to a Charles and Francis Hunter crusade in Cobo Hall, Detroit on a Saturday night. My wife Joanne and daughters already had the gift of tongues. At the end of the service the invitation was given for those who sought the gift of tongues, I went forward and in the midst of the packed assembly, all praying in tongues, the Holy Spirit gave me utterance in tongues that was such a blessing; the presence of the Holy Spirit and of Jesus was so real that I fell on my knees and wept praising the Lord in tongues. Since, that day I love to approach the throne of God in prayer, speaking in the Holy Spirit's language to present my prayers before the throne of God. I know that God has also given to some the gift of interpreting tongues but that is not my gift. But, oh what edifying power is experienced when the Holy Spirit speaks through me to God in the Name of Jesus in the language of heaven. It is so soul searching and refreshes my spirit.

DIVERSITY OF THE GIFTS OF THE HOLY SPIRIT

I Corinthians 12:4-6 speak about the work of the Holy Spirit in the diversities (various kinds) of gifts, "Now there are diversities of gifts, but the same Spirit. It also speaks about the different ministries of our Lord Jesus Christ, "And there are differences of administrations (ministries), but the same Lord". It also speaks of the diversities of operations (activities) the energo or working power of God through His Holy Spirit of Truth, "And the manifestation of the Spirit is given to every man to profit withal (all-everyone in Christ)". The Holy Spirit is the oil, unction or anointing power that fuels the flames of Christianity. Then versus 8-10 lists the various gifts of the Holy Spirit. The Greek word used here for gifts is charisma: a God given endowment or miraculous faculty (ability, aptitude, power); the dunamis (omnipotent authority) and energo (energized working) power of God manifested through His Holy Spirit of Truth.

THE HOLY SPIRIT'S GIFT OF GOD'S WORD OF WISDOM

"For to one is given by the Spirit the Word of Wisdom (Greek Sophia). This Wisdom is from God and is defined as: spiritual instruction; Spirit revealed knowledge of God and His Divine Nature; God given skills and ability to know and do the will of God effectively. That is why we are to listen to the Holy Spirit and allow Him to speak through us in times of satanic opposition and adversities of life. In Proverbs 1:23 Wisdom speaks, "Turn you at my reproof: behold, I will pour out My Spirit unto you, I will make known My Words unto you. These are God's Words of power, promise, purpose and provision. Proverbs are God's inspired maxims or Word of Truth. Proverbs 2:1-22 speaks of the necessity to heed the Wisdom of God. "My son, if you will receive My Words, and hide (treasure) My commandments with you; so that you will incline your ear unto (My) Wisdom, and apply your heart (spirit) to understanding; Yea, if you will cry after (thirst) for knowledge, and lift up your voice (earnest desire) for understanding; If you seek her as silver, and search for her as hid treasures; Then you shall understand the fear (reverential awe) of the Lord, and find the knowledge of God. For the Lord gives (to us) Wisdom: out of His mouth comes knowledge and understanding. He is ready to give His sound Wisdom to His righteous ones: He is a shield to them that walk uprightly. He keeps (guards His paths of justice and preserves or delivers His saints in His way, righteousness. Psalm 91 confirms this truth and in verse 15-16 promises, "He (His saints) shall call upon Me, and I will answer him: I will be with him in trouble; I will deliver him, and honor him. With long life I will satisfy him, and show him my salvation".

THE HOLY SPIRIT'S GIFT OF THE WORD OF KNOWLEDGE

The word used in I Corinthians 12::8 for knowledge is gnosis which refers to an especial kind of knowledge: the knowledge of God and His Christ, Jesus. It is the same word used in Luke 11:52 as "the key of knowledge". It unlocks the treasure chest of the mystery of the ages concerning God's Son, Jesus, "To whom God would make known what is the riches of the glory of this mystery among the gentiles (unbelievers); which is Christ in you, the hope of glory". The knowledge of Christ in you (us) the Hope of Glory would make us cry out as Paul in Philippians 3:10, "That I may know Him, and the power of His resurrection, and the fellowship of His sufferings, being made conformable unto His death". Oh, what a revelation that would be, to know Him, Jesus the Christ as the Son of God and as the Son of man in His resurrection power which includes our Redemption fulfilled; to know Him in His passion, His suffering and thoughts for me; to know Him as I conform (to be by His power made like Him) to His image! The totality of His stature!

In II Peter 1:1-4 Peter writes, "to them that have obtained like (the same kind of) faith with us through the righteousness of (our) God and our Saviour Jesus Christ: Grace and peace be multiplied unto you through the knowledge of God, and of Jesus our Lord. According as His Divine Power has given unto us all things that pertain unto life and godliness, through the knowledge of Him that has called us to (in) glory and virtue: Whereby are given unto us exceeding great and precious promises: that by these you might be partakers of the Divine Nature, having escaped he corruption that is in the world through lust". Then in verse 8 Peter affirms, "For if these things (fruit of the Spirit of verses 5-7) be in you, and abound (super abound-more than enough), they (shall) make you to be neither barren nor unfruitful in the knowledge of our Lord Jesus Christ". This refers to the knowledge of Christ represented by the fruit of the Spirit of Galatians 5:22, "Love, Joy, Peace, Longsuffering, Gentleness, Goodness, Faithfulness, Meekness and Temperance".

THE GIFT OF THE HOLY SPIRIT: OUR SUPERNATURAL FAITH

This refers to the unction (anointing) of Christ through the power of the Holy Spirit to believe the Word of God in all that He is as the Son of God and all that He is as the Son of man. As stated previously, faith cannot operate without love, so our faith begins with our love for God and Jesus the Lord with all of our being: all our heart (spirit); all of our soul; all of our mind; and all of our strength (body); and our neighbor as ourselves (a way to love God through our love for others) Luke 10:27.

I Corinthians 12:9 says that the manifestation of the Holy Spirit by which mankind is profited is faith, "To another (the gift of) faith by the same Spirit". The word used here for faith is pistis: faith, belief, firm persuasion. It is derived from peitho which means that the Holy Spirit is active in (His energy that promotes) our faith: in belief; assurance; conviction; salvation; fruits of the Spirit; revelation of Truth; Inspiration of the Word of God; faithfulness; activities of Christ in us. It is the Holy Spirit that energizes our God given faith and persuades (draws) us to yield to those things that He presents to our hearts and minds concerning God and Christ.

John 16:13-15 reveals this to us, "Howbeit when He (the Holy Spirit), the Spirit of Truth, is come, He will guide you into all truth: for He shall not speak of Himself; but whatsoever He shall hear (from the Father, God through Jesus Christ the Son), that shall He speak: and He will show you things to come. He shall glorify Me: for He shall receive of (what is) mine, and shall show it unto you (the children of God). All things that the Father has are mine: therefore said I, that He (Holy Spirit) shall take of mine (that which Christ received from the Father) and shall show it unto you".

THE GIFTS OF THE HOLY SPIRIT IN HEALING

Another gift of the Holy Spirit is that of the power to heal, "to another (individually) the gifts of healing by the same (Holy) Spirit" I Corinthians 12:9b). Notice it says, "Gifts of healing" denoting that there are different kinds of healing. Even Jesus demonstrated this when: at times he healed individuals; other times he healed a group of individuals (lepers); again he healed a blind man by anointing his eyes with His spittle and clay and the man's obedience of washing in the pool of Siloam; on another occasion Jesus heals a deaf and dumb man (impediment of speech) when he spit and touched the man's tongue with His finger and putting his fingers into his ears and praying to His Father in Heaven, "be opened" and "straightway (immediately) the man's ears were opened, and the string of his tongue was loosed, and he spake plain"; then Jesus said to a man at the pool of Bethesda and the palsied man let down through the roof before Jesus, by his friends, "Arise, and take up thy bed and walk".

Jesus healed through the faith of the recipient who came to Jesus in Faith, as the woman with the issue of blood who touched the hem of his cloak. The Anointing virtue of Jesus was keenly felt when the woman with the plague of an issue of blood, by faith touched Jesus and "virtue" (healing power) responding to the faith of the woman, emanated from Jesus. Jesus healed Jairus' (ruler of the Synagogue) daughter even though she died before Jesus came to her. Jesus said unto him, "Be not afraid, only believe" (have faith). Jesus also healed Mary Magdalene and the Gadarene demoniac and many others by casting out devils (demons-angels of hell and servants of Satan). The Word plainly reveals that Jesus healed all who came to Him by faith, believing to receive from him their healing. Matthew 4:23-24 says, "And Jesus went about all Galilee, teaching in their synagogues, and preaching the gospel of the Kingdom, and healing all manner of sickness and all manner of disease among the people. And His fame went throughout all Syria and they brought unto Him all sick people that were taken with divers (various) diseases and torments, and those which were possessed with devils (demons), and those which were lunatic (epileptics), and those that had the palsy (were paralyzed); and He healed them (all)".

Therefore, the gifts of the Spirit are given to every son or daughter in Christ Jesus, individually for various purposes and in diver's manners (ways). I remember seeing Kathryn Kuhlman heal with such convincing power of the Holy Spirit in action (energo working power of the Holy Spirit) that just watching made one feel the awesome power of God as many were healed. She believed in the miraculous healing power of God such as the raising of the dead as Jesus did for Lazarus. Then, what a life Smith Wigglesworth lived as a friend of the Holy Spirit. The working power of the Holy Spirit worked mightily through him as he without reservation believed in the power of the Holy Spirit to heal. He believed that God has made it possible for all of the sons and daughters of God to walk in divine health and wholeness of living. By the laying on of hands; by the touch of faith we can be instruments of healing in the power of the Holy Spirit of Truth.

THE HOLY SPIRITS GIFT OF MIRACLES

I Corinthians 12:10 begins, "To another (individuals) the working of miracles" reveals the power of the Holy Spirit through the sons and daughters of God in the demonstration of the miracles of God. The word used here for miracles is dunamis or miraculous power of God. It is used in I Corinthians 12:28, "And God has set some in the church, first apostles, secondarily prophets, thirdly teachers, after that miracles (dunamis), then gifts of healings, helps, governments, diversities of tongues". Also God bore witness to those who received His so great salvation, "God also bearing them witness, both with signs and wonders, and with divers (various) miracles (dunamis), and gifts of the Holy Ghost (Spirit), according to His own will" (Hebrews 2:4). In my own words, I believe that a Divine demonstration of a miracle of God is the manifestation of His absolute authority as God in the extraordinary (supernatural) use and visible display of His power for His righteous purpose: the benefit of His beloved sons and daughters of Light.

THE HOLY SPIRIT'S GIFT OF PROPHESY

Again I Corinthians 12:10, in speaking of another gift of the Holy Spirit states, "to another prophecy". It is the word prophetes which refers to a prophet or one divinely commissioned or anointed to preach the message of God. It also refers to a teacher of revealed and divinely inspirited Truth. It is also the one given a message of God to preach and teach the truth of God's Word with zealous diligence. Paul said in I Corinthians 9:16, "For though I preach the Gospel (message of salvation), I have nothing to glory of; for necessity is laid upon me; yea, woe is unto me, if I preach not the Gospel". The flames of the Holy Spirit that came upon Jesus disciples on Pentecost Sunday in the upper room enfolded and indwelt them and became a burning desire and passion within their spirit to preach and teach and herald the Word of God, of salvation to the uttermost for everyone who would believe.

The message of the Holy Spirit to each of the churches listed in the Church dispensation (stewardship) from Christ to the end of the age is revealed in Revelation chapters 2 and 3. It is a message of commendation and condemnation for their work or lack of it, in the Spirit during their particular age (dispensation) of service notated by the seven churches. It is also an exhortation to hear (know and understand) what the Spirit is saying unto them. After each message of the Holy Spirit to the church the admonition is given, "He that has an ear (physical and spiritual ear), let him hear what the Spirit says unto the churches; "to him (the individuals of the body of Christ) that overcomes (the world system with its sinful lawlessness under the leadership of Satan) will I give to eat of the tree of life" (Ephesus); "should not be hurt of the second death" (Smyrna); "to eat of the hidden manna and I will give him a white stone with a new name written (denoting acceptance and God's approval " (Pergamos); "the morning star" (Thyatira); "shall be clothed with white raiment (Christ's righteousness)and I will not blot his name out of the book of life, but will confess his name before my Father , and before the angels" (of heaven)" (Sardis); "I will make a pillar in the temple of My God, and he shall go no more out; and I will write upon him the name of My God, and the name of the city of My God, which is the New Jerusalem, which comes down out of heaven from My God: and I will write upon him my new name" (Philadelphia); "to sit with Me in My throne, even as I also overcame and am set down with My father in (on) His throne" (Laodicea).

The whole of the Word of God is the inspired (breathed out) message of God given through His Holy Spirit of Truth. All of the statements such as "Thus saith the Lord"; the word of the Lord came"; It is written"; As the Holy Spirit saith"; According to scripture"; and "All scripture is given by inspiration of God" is referring to the prophetic ministry of the Holy Spirit. In all of the fulfilled prophesy, miracles, teachings, revelations, mysteries, instructions written authority of God from Genesis to Revelation is by inspiration of the Holy Spirit. All of the writers of the

Holy Scriptures, the Word of God were the amanuenses or secretaries of the Holy Spirit who wrote verbatim what was dictated by God through the Holy Spirit of Truth.

GIFT OF THE HOLY SPIRIT IN DISCERNING OF SPIRITS

The Spirit world consists of God Himself who is Spirit, Jesus Christ His son and the Holy Spirit of Truth. It also consists of the angels whom God created: all of the hosts of heaven and those who voluntarily rebelled with Satan and were cast down to earth and later to a place prepared for them by God, the Abyss of Hell. It essence it also refers to mankind as we were created by God through Jesus Christ His Word of life, as spirit beings receiving the breath of God within a body formed by God, thus becoming finite beings of this earth. Someday, our soul (spirit) will return to God in a glorified body, even as Jesus Christ when He was resurrected. When we are redeemed, we shall be like Him in His resurrection and glorification.

In I John 2:20-22 John through the inspiration of the Holy Spirit reveals, "But you (the sons and daughters of God) have an unction (anointing of the Holy Spirit) from the Holy One, and ye know all things. I have not written unto you because you know not the truth, but because you know it, and that no lie is of the truth. Who is a liar but he that denies that Jesus is the Christ? He is antichrist that denies the Father and the Son". The discerning of spirits is necessary because of the antichrists (those possessed by the spirit of evil, darkness, Satan) who denied that Jesus is the Son of God, God's Christ (Messiah) and Savior of the world.

I John 4:1-6 more emphatically address the discernment of spirits, "Beloved, believe not every spirit, but try (test, examine) the spirits whether they are of God: because many false prophets (possessed by the spirit of antichrist) are gone out into the world. Hereby know you that Spirit of God: Every spirit that confesses that Jesus Christ is come in the flesh is of God. And every spirit that confesses not that Jesus Christ is come in the flesh is not of God: and this is that spirit of antichrist, whereof you have heard that it should come; and even now already is in the world. Ye are of God, little children, and have overcome them: because greater is He that is in you (the Holy Spirit), than he (Satan) that is in the world. They (antichrists) are of the world (system under Satan's power and influence) therefore speak they of the world (the things associated with Satan's domain), and the world hears them (Satan's voice through his demon angels). We are of God: he that knows God hears us; he that is not of God hears not us. Hereby we know (the difference between) the spirit of truth, and the spirit of error".

Even Solomon, in his wisdom when he became King asked God for an understanding heart that would enable him to discern between the spirit of good and the spirit of evil (I Kings 3:9). David prayed that his spiritual eyes may see (discern) the goodness of God through His law (Psalm 119:18). Daniel sought discernment (interpretive insight) of the dream he had concerning the four beasts (Daniel 7:16). I Corinthians 2:14-16 reveals, "But the natural man (one who knows not God) receives not the things of the Spirit (Holy Spirit) of God: for they are foolishness unto him: neither can he know them, because they are spiritually discerned (can only be understood through the indwelling of His Holy Spirit). But he that is spiritual (filled with the Holy Spirit) judges (understands the spiritual significance of) all things, yet he himself is judged (Greek anakrino, scrutinized or called into question) of no man. For who has known the mind of the Lord, that he may instruct Him? But we have the mind of Christ".

THE HOLY SPIRIT'S GIFT OF DIVERS KINDS OF TONGUES

The diverse composition of tongues as presented in the Word of God is given by the Holy Spirit of Truth and when one experiences any one kind of "tongues" he knows that it is given by the Holy Spirit for the purpose of Gods revelation and edification of truth in this world. It can be in the form of a known language as all languages of the world are lingual (spoken with the use of the tongue). It can be used by the Holy Spirit to speak the gospel message to someone who does not have prior knowledge of that language. It is spoken through the sons and daughters of God by the Holy Spirit who searches the deep things of God and takes the thoughts and intents of our heart, which we are not able to express and bring it before the throne of God as a petition, supplication or request in prayer.

Jesus said in Mark 16:17-18, "These signs shall follow them that believe; In My name shall they cast out devils (demons-Satan's host of hell); they shall speak with new tongues; They shall take up serpents, and they drink any deadly thing it shall not hurt them; they shall lay hands on the sick, and they shall recover." New tongues in that it was a language new to the possessor, for it is the language of the Holy Spirit that speaks in behalf of the believer unto God.

All that God gives to us through the Holy Spirit is for our edification, our maturity or growing up into the stature of Christ. God gave to us the Holy Spirit because the Holy Spirit is God with us, His presence within us and it is our hope of glory in Christ Jesus our Lord. It is the love of God dwelling in our hearts by faith. It is being rooted and grounded in His Love. It is knowing the breadth, length, depth and height of His love that continually surrounds us filling us withal of His fullness" (Ephesians 3:17-19).

I Corinthians 12:11 is best explained by the Amplified Bible text, "All these (gifts, achievements, abilities) are inspired and brought to pass by one and the same (Holy) Spirit, Who apportions to each person individually (exactly) as He chooses".

CHAPTER ELEVEN

GOD'S LOVE MANIFESTED IN HIS SONS AND DAUGHTERS

LOVE, THE WAY OF EXCELLENCE

In speaking of the body of Christ, the church, Paul says, "Now you are the body of Christ, and members in particular (individually). And God has set some in the church (appointed these), first apostles, secondarily prophets, thirdly teachers, after that miracles, then gifts of healings, helps, governments, diversities of tongues. Are all apostles? Are all prophets? Are all teachers? Are all workers of miracles? Have all gifts of healing? Do all speak with tongues? Do all interpret (tongues)? But covet (desire) earnestly the best gifts and yet show I unto you a more excellent way" (I Corinthians 12:27-31). Colossians 3:14 tells us the more excellent way is love the bond of perfectness.

All the gifts of the Holy Spirit operate through love just as all of the law and prophets are summed up or accomplished through loving God with our whole heart mind, soul, and body and our neighbor as ourselves (Matthew 22:39-40). The Love chapter of the word of God, I Corinthians 13:1-13 gives us God's prerequisite of unfeigned (without hypocrisy) love. I Peter 1:22 exhorts us, "Seeing you have purified your souls in obeying the truth through the Spirit unto unfeigned (sincere) love of the brethren, see that you love one another with a pure heart fervently".

Paul was eloquent in speech, but His power of prophecy (preaching) came from the Holy Spirit. Thus, Paul begins I Corinthians chapter 13, "Though I speak with the tongues (language) of men and of angels (of earth and heaven), and have not charity (love), I am become as a sounding brass, or a tinkling (clanging) cymbal (loud noise without harmony or understanding), and though I have the gift of prophecy, and understand all mysteries, and all knowledge; and though I have all faith, so that I could remove mountains, and have not charity (love), I am nothing".

Then in verse four Paul reveals the nature and character of Jesus as he says, "love suffers long and is kind; love envies not; love does not brag or boast; is not arrogant; is not rude; seeks not its own way; is not easily provoked; thinks no evil of any neighbor; does not rejoice in iniquity but rejoices in the truth; endures all things; and believes in all things that are of faith. That is why we are beseeched to "be like Jesus". Paul goes on to say that love never fails to accomplish its objective. Love is as God for God is love: it prevailed yesterday (eternity before creation); it prevails today; and it will prevail in eternity to come. In fact, Paul reveals to our hearts that both faith and hope, although important in Gods purpose for our life, operate by love's perfect bonding power (Colossians 3:14). We become one with Christ in Love.

In John 13:34-35 Jesus explains to His sons and daughters of faith, "A new commandment (in that it is now Jesus commandment or binding request) I give to you, that you love one another; as I have loved you, that you also love one another. By this shall all men (everyone) know that you are (indeed) my disciples, if you have love one to another". Jesus loved the little children and demonstrated it as recorded in Mark 10:13-14, "And they brought young children to Him (Jesus), that he should touch them: and His disciples rebuked those that brought them. But when Jesus saw it, He was much displeased, and said unto them, 'Suffer (allow) the little children to come unto me, and forbid them not: for of such is the kingdom of God".

In John 11:35-36, "'Jesus wept (openly and passionately cried out). Then said the Jews, 'Behold how He (Jesus) loved him' (Lazarus)!" How appropriate that Jesus would use the penmanship of His beloved, John to write about such love such wondrous love. This kind of love in us can only come from our Father in Heaven through the shed blood of Jesus on Calvary and ministered in and through us by the blessed Holy Spirit of Truth. All who professes the name of Jesus should manifest this love to the extent that we can love our enemies (not be like them) and be merciful to those who have need of the mercy of God. Love is longsuffering toward others as Christ suffered long on the Cross for our salvation.

The world system is one of hate and self-indulgence and self-promotion at the expense of others. It is a manifestation of the prince of this world, Satan, who wanted to promote himself above God (Isaiah 14:12-15).

Even under the guise of religious fervor, the world seethes with hate and murderous vindictiveness.

CHAPTER TWELVE

GOD'S LOVE MANIFESTED IN HIS BLESSINGS

THE BLESSINGS OF OBEDIENCE

Deuteronomy 28:1-9 is God's message to His elect, "And it shall come to pass, if you will hearken (listen) diligently to the voice of the Lord your God, to observe and to do all His commandments which I (He) commands you this day, that the Lord your God will set (place) you on High above all nations of the earth. And all these blessings shall come on you, and overtake (possess) you, if you will harken unto the voice of the Lord your God. Blessed you shall be in the city, and blessed you shall be in the field. Blessed shall be the fruit (offspring) of your body, and the fruit of your ground (produce); and the fruit of you cattle, the increase of your kine (cattle), and the flocks of your sheep. Blessed you shall be in your basket (bread container) and in your store (kneading bowl). (You will be) blessed when you come in, and blessed you will be when you go out. The Lord shall cause your enemies that rise up against you to be smitten before your face: they shall come out against thee one way, and flee before you seven ways. The Lord shall command the blessing upon you in your storehouses (warehouses) and in all that you set your hand to do; and He shall bless you in the land which the Lord our God gives to you".

It is when we obey or bless the Lord God Almighty that He blesses us. In the Old Testament the Hebrew word for bless is barak, a primary root word that means to kneel or to bless God in an act of adoration and praise. In the New Testament it is the Greek word eulogia from which the English word eulogize (to speak well of, praise, glorify) is derived. The American Heritage Dictionary states that the world bless, blessed or blest means to make holy by religious rite; sanctify; honor as holy; glorify; bless the Lord; and to invoke divine favor. The blessed individual is one who enjoys happiness, a state of being contented, that all is well between God and me.

The psalmist David upon meditating upon the blessings of His Lord God Jehovah wrote Psalm 103:1-5, "Bless the Lord, O my soul: and all that is within me bless His Holy Name. Bless the Lord, O my soul, and forget not all His benefits (blessings): Who forgives all my iniquities; Who heals all my diseases; Who redeems my life from destruction; Who crowns (Anointing cover) you with (His) loving-kindness and tender mercies; Who satisfies my mouth with good things; so that my youth is renewed like the eagle's. The good things are associated with Jesus Christ in that in communion we eat the Bread of Life: sustenance and nourishment of His flesh; and His Blood: God's Covenant of reconciliation within us. I Peter 2:3 states, "If so be ye have tasted that the Lord is gracious". To taste of the Lord or spiritual things is to perceive, feed on, or experience the truth of Him and His Word of Truth. Jeremiah 17:7 reveals, "Blessed is the man or (woman) what trusts in the Lord, and whose hope is in the Lord". God is more than able to "do exceeding abundantly above all that we ask or think, according to the power that works in us" (Ephesians 3:20).

BLESSED ART THOU

Jesus Sermon on the mount (Matthew 5), the Beatitudes speaks about the blessedness (joy unspeakable and full of glory) of mankind in serving God. To be blessed of God is to be happy, full of joy that is within the spirit and soul of every believer in God through Christ Jesus our Lord. "Blessed are the poor in spirit: for theirs is the Kingdom of Heaven". These are the spiritually poor (your and my former condition before receiving Jesus as Lord and Savior) who when they receive Jesus as Lord and Savior become spiritually rich and inherit all of the Kingdom of Heaven. "Blessed are they that mourn: for they shall be comforted" speaks of Jesus love in bringing joy and peace and blessing to those who partake of His grace in salvation. The Amplified Bible reads, "Blessed and enviably happy (with a happiness produced by the experience of God's favor and especially conditioned by the revelation of His matchless grace) are those who mourn, for they shall be comforted". "Blessed are the meek for they shall inherit the earth". The meek are those who have submitted and humbled themselves before God and who have enjoyed the favor of God in salvation. They are mild, patient, longsuffering, and they shall inherit heaven and earth. "Blessed are they who hunger and thirsts after righteousness: for they shall be filled".

Isaiah 55:1 bids us, "Ho, every one that thirsts, come you to the waters (of life), and he that has no money; come you, buy, and eat; yea, come buy wine and milk without money and without price". Jesus the bread of life and the fountain of living waters will open up His vast storehouse of good things. "Blessed are the merciful: for they shall obtain mercy". These are those who have obtained God's mercy in Salvation and desire to extend that mercy to others. "Blessed are the peacemakers: for they shall be called the children of God". There is no peace of mind or spirit in the world of turmoil and unrest, but God extends His peace that passes all understanding to His children who in turn proclaim the message of peace through Jesus Christ the Prince of Peace. "Blessed are they which are persecuted for righteousness sake: for there is the Kingdom of Heaven". II Timothy 3:12 states, "Yea, and all that will live godly in Christ Jesus shall suffer persecution". But, Romans 8:35 & 37 questions and answers, "Who shall separate us from the love of Christ? Shall tribulation, or distress, or persecution, or famine, or nakedness, or peril, or sword? Nay, in all these things we are more than conquerors through Him that loved us". Then Jesus commands us to, "Rejoice, and be exceeding glad: for great is your reward in Heaven: for so persecuted they the prophets which were before you". We are the salt (healing preservative) of the earth and we are the light (illuminating power in the darkness) of the world.

GOD'S BLESSING OF SALVATION

God so loved the world that He gave to us His gift of love, Jesus, His only begotten Son, that whosoever believes in Him should not perish with the sinful and ungodly together with Satan and His grotesque demons, but have everlasting life.

GOD'S BLESSING OF ELECTION

"Blessed be the God and Father of our Lord Jesus Christ, Who has blessed us with all spiritual blessings in heavenly Places in Christ:

according as He has chosen us in Him before the foundation of the world, that we should be holy and without blame before Him in love: Having predestinated us unto the adoption of children (sons and daughters) by Jesus Christ to Himself, according to the good pleasure of His will" (Ephesians 1:3-5).

GOD'S BLESSING OF REGENERATION

"Therefore if any man be in Christ, he is a new creation: old things are passed away: behold, all things are become new" (II Corinthians 5:27).

GOD'S BLESSING IN HIS FORGIVENESS

"Who (God) has delivered us from the power of darkness, and has translated us into the Kingdom of His dear Son: In Whom we have redemption through His blood, even the forgiveness of sins" (Colossians 1:13-14).

GOD'S BLESSING IN OUR ADOPTION

"For we have not received the spirit of bondage again to fear, but we have received the Spirit (Holy Spirit) of adoption, whereby we cry, Abba, Father. The Spirit itself bears witness with our spirit, that we are the children of God" (Romans 8:15-16).

GOD'S BLESSING IN FREEDOM FROM CONDEMNATION

"There is therefore now no condemnation to them which are in Christ Jesus, who walk not after the flesh, but after the Spirit" (Romans 8:1).

GOD'S BLESSING IN GIVING TO US THE HOLY SPIRIT

"But you shall receive power, after (when) that the Holy Spirit is come upon you: and you shall be witness unto me both in Jerusalem, and in all Judea, and in Samaria, and unto the uttermost part of the earth" (Acts 1:8).

GOD'S BLESSING IN OUR JUSTIFICATION

When we were justified in Christ Jesus, we were made righteous before the throne of God. Romans 4:25 says, "Who (Jesus) was delivered for (because of) our offenses (sins), and was raised again for our justification". Then Romans 5:18, "Therefore as by the offense (sin) of one (Adam) judgment came upon all men to condemnation; even so by the righteousness of one (Jesus) the free gift came upon all men unto justification of life". We are made righteous through the shed blood and resurrection of our Lord and Savior Jesus Christ.

GOD'S BLESSING IN OUR NEW COVENANT

This new covenant is a gift (blessing) of God in that God initiation the action and Jesus blood was the atoning sacrifice. His Holy Spirit is the earnest (seal of assurance) that this covenant will never be broken by God and is everlasting. Jesus Christ Himself is our High Priest and Mediator of this New Covenant. We refer to the Old Testament as the Old Covenant of God and the New Testament as the New Covenant of God. It is a Testament in that it is God's own faithful testimony to His own elect, both of the Jews and the gentile who are redeemed by faith in the blood sacrifice and resurrection of Jesus as Lord and Savior. Hebrews 8:6-13 reveals to us that it is a more excellent ministry, by a better mediator (the Son of God) established upon better promises. God in the New Covenant (Testament) put His laws within our heart (spirit) and mind (soul), the presence of the Holy Spirit. In His Mercy God has blessed us with access to His Throne by the way of Jesus Christ His Son.

GOD'S LOVE AND BLESSING REVEALED IN HIS CHASTISEMENT

Hebrews 12:5-11 reveals these words of the Lord, "And you have forgotten the exhortation (of God) which speaks unto you as unto children (sons and daughters of God). My son, despise not the chastening of the Lord, nor faint (be discouraged) when you are rebuked (disciplined) of Him. For whom the Lord so loves He chastens, and scourges (disciplines) every son (or daughter) whom He receives. If you endure chastening, God deals with you as with sons, for what son is he whom the Father chastens not? But if you be without chastisement (correction), whereof all are partakers (all children of God share or are subject to), then are ye bastards (illegitimate), and not sons. Furthermore, we have had fathers of our flesh which corrected us, and we gave them reverence: shall we not much rather be in subjection unto the Father of spirits (our spirit) and live? For they (our earthly father) verily for a few days chastened us after their pleasure (desire to see me as a son to be proud of); but He (God) for our profit that we might be partakers of His holiness. Now no chastening for the present seems to be joyous, but grievous: nevertheless afterward it yields the peaceable fruit of righteousness unto them which are exercised (lovingly corrected) thereby".

I well remember my father's correction and discipline when I stepped out of harmony with his instructions of good behavior and began to dabble into the sinful elements of this world. I loved my father and had the fear of respect for his voice of guidance. At the age of 87 I am ever grateful for his loving hand of correction and sage words of wisdom".

GOD'S BLESSING (LOVE) MANIFESTED IN OUR SANCTIFICATION

It is through the blood, the word and the Spirit of God that we are sanctified (separated unto God through Christ Jesus) by God Himself, for we are the, "Elect according to the foreknowledge of God the Father, through sanctification of the Spirit, unto obedience and sprinkling of the blood of Jesus Christ".

GOD'S BLESSING REVEALED IN OUR GLORIFICATION

Romans 8:30 reveals, "Moreover whom He (God) did predestinate, them He also called: and whom He called, them He also justified (made righteous): and whom He justified, them He also glorified". Glorification has a number of interrelated definitions in both the English dictionary and Greek concordance, but here it refers to our redemption, when our bodies are raised incorruptible and we are changed into a body like Him, Jesus who made it possible. A glorious body fit for His glory. Here it is used in the past tense (glorified) signifying that when we were predestined, when we received Jesus blood sacrifice as our Lord and Savior, we were already destined for His glory.

Thus, "all things work together for good (are blessed) to them that love God, to them who are the called according to His purpose" (Romans 8:28).

CHAPTER THIRTEEN

GOD'S LOVE REVEALED IN HIS GRACE

AMAZING GRACE MANIFESTED BY AMAZING LOVE

One of my favorite hymns is "Amazing Grace" written by one, John Newton who experienced the grace of God in Salvation. A ship captain of a slave ship who did despicable things being involved in the slave trade, found Jesus who washed away all of his sin and cleansed him of the stench and degradation of slave trafficking. It is his testimony of God's grace. In his song of testimony and praise he emphatically reveals the meaning of grace: "Amazing grace (of God) how sweet the sound! That saved a wretch like me! I once was lost, but now am found; was blind, but now I see. Twas (it was) grace that taught my heart to fear, and grace my fears relieved. How precious did that grace appear, the hour I first believed! Thro' many dangers, toils, and snares, I have already come. 'Tis grace that brought me safe thus far and grace will lead me home. When we've been there ten thousand years, Bright, shining as the sun, we've no less days to sing God's praise than when we first begun".

God's grace is greater than all of our sin, for it is God's Divine favor or blessing that His love manifests and demonstrates to us in spite of our sinfulness. Romans 5:8 affirms, "But God commended (demonstrated) His love toward us, in that, while we were yet sinners, Christ died for us".

As stated previously the Greek word for Grace is Charisma which is akin to the Hebrew word shalowm or shalom. Both are used for greetings of friendship and love. Paul addresses his letters to the churches with "Grace and Peace be multiplied unto you." Shalom is a greeting which desires that the one addressed would enjoy a life of peace, safety, happiness, well-being, good health and prosperity. Grace also salutes the one so addressed with joy, gladness, wholeness, health, well-being, peace, the benefits of God's favor, God's benevolent lovingkindness and His Omnipresent guardianship of our spirit, soul and body (I Thessalonians 5:23).

Take the whole of God's Word, the Bible from Genesis to Revelations; from His creative fiat throughout the scriptural history of mankind; from His manifestations and provisions throughout the dispensation of church history; throughout the pages of His New Covenant: Jesus Christ His Son as the Son of man, His life of healing and miracles, His suffering, His shedding of His precious blood, His burial and Resurrection and gift of salvation to whosoever will and His promise of redemption and eternal life. You would only be able to begin to see, to perceive, to visualize, to experience, to know the Grace of God.

GOD'S GRACE AND SALVATION

God's grace is synonymous with His Love for His grace includes His Love. "For by Grace are you saved through faith; and not of yourselves: it is the gift of God" (Ephesians 2:8). John 3:16 tells us that God so loved us that He gave His only begotten Son as His gift of love for us so we could spend eternity in the secret place of His heavenly realm called heaven.

Ephesians 2:5 reveals, "Even when we were dead in sins, (He, God) has quickened us (made us alive) together with Christ, (by grace are you - you have been saved ;)" and Ephesians 2:8 reaffirms, "For by grace are you (you have been) saved through faith; and that not of yourselves: it is the gift of God". That Grace is the basis of our salvation is revealed in these words, "In Whom (Jesus) we have redemption through His blood, the forgiveness of sins, according to the riches of His grace".

Only God's grace can explain why or how sinful mankind, bound for hell can inherit God's Holy Heaven. Paul the persecutor of the church of God and instrumental in the execution of Christians, God's people, obtained God's Grace and Mercy and became God's chosen Apostle to the gentiles. He was changed when he recognized that it was Jesus he was really persecuting and gave himself to Jesus and received Jesus as his Lord and Savior with these words, "What will you have me to do, Lord?" found in Acts 9:6.

GOD'S GRACE OPERATIVE IN OUR FAITH

As referred to previously Ephesians 2:8 states, "For by grace are you saved through faith; and that not of yourselves: it is the gift of God". Romans 4:16 reveals that promise of righteousness in Christ Jesus through faith was a gift of God's grace, "Therefore it is of faith, that it might be by (according to) grace; to the end the promise might be sure to all the seed (of Abraham, both Jew and Gentile); not to that only which is of the law, but to that also which is of the faith of Abraham; who is the father of us all" (in faith).

Grace and Faith work together. Paul wrote in Romans 5:1-2, "Therefore being justified by faith, we have peace with God through our Lord Jesus Christ: By Whom (Jesus finished work on the Cross of Calvary) also we have access by faith into this grace wherein we stand, and rejoice in hope of the glory of God".

GOD'S GRACE IN OUR JUSTIFICATION

It is only by God's Grace that we are justified, for without God's unmerited favor in our behalf, we would not warrant being justified (made righteous) before God, "For all have sinned, and come short of the glory of God; Being justified freely by His grace through the redemption that is in Christ Jesus" (Romans 5:23-24). God's Grace made it possible for Jesus to be our propitiation (God's only Son as the Son of man with the power to appease the wrath of God against sin) through His shed blood. As our propitiation, Jesus expiated or appeased God's Holy requirement of the Law, that the wages of sin is death (Romans 6:23) and since all have sinned and come short of God's glory (Romans 3:23), His grace allowed us (mankind) to be reconciled back to Him (God) and through Jesus Resurrection we were then justified, made completely righteous. All this was made possible by our faith through God's Grace.

GOD'S GRACE AND HIS FORGIVENESS

Ephesians 1:7 states, "In Whom (Jesus) we have redemption through His blood, the forgiveness of sins, according to the riches of His grace". The riches of His Grace is His will (His design and purpose) making known to us that everything He has done and is doing in the dispensation of the fullness of times are all through His Son Jesus in Whom we have obtained an inheritance. And it is all for our benefit that God works (energizes and consummates His will through the Holy Spirit) all things for His praise, honor and glory through His heirs of righteousness, His sons and daughters in Christ Jesus. Forgiveness is taking our sin and covering it by the blood of Jesus which completely blots it out, eradicates it, leaving no proof that it ever existed. We are washed (cleansed) white as snow; no taint of sin, no reeking smell of sin, no taste of sin, no effects of sin, no more bondage or yoke of being a slave to sin: free to live the abundant life in Christ Jesus our Lord and Savior. His Grace is rich in that it is God's abundant and bountiful benefits that flow from God to us through His Son, Jesus. Therefore, "If we confess our sins, He (God) is faithful and just to forgive us our sins and to cleanse us from all unrighteousness" (I John 1:9).

A SPIRIT MANIFESTED VIEW OF GOD'S GRACE

God's Grace is all-abundant in that it covers every exigency of life and the sin that so easily beset (ensnare) us. Romans 5:15-18 reveals to us that through Adam's disobedience and sin all of humanity became tainted (all were under the penalty of death) bringing judgment and condemnation: but in Christ, through His shed blood, redemption and justification; reconciliation was extended by God to all humanity and we obtained life through Christ's obedience to His Father's will. However, we must of our own free will receive the grace of God through faith in Jesus Christ as our Savior and Lord.

God's Grace is all-sufficient, "And He (Jesus) said unto me, 'My grace is sufficient for thee: for my strength (power) is made perfect in weakness. Most gladly therefore will I rather glory in my infirmities (weaknesses), that the power of Christ may rest upon me". This statement is derived from Paul's discussion with the Lord concerning his "thorn in the flesh" (Satan's oppression). It is more important to note here that God's Grace is sufficient (more than enough) for every contingency of life. When we as finite beings are weak in the flesh and look to Jesus our High Priest for help in time of need, His power is more than sufficient for our every desire or requirement of life.

God's Grace is manifested in the greatness of God's power. Acts 4:33 states, "And with great power gave the apostles witness (testified) of the resurrection of the Lord Jesus: and great grace was upon them all". With great power, ability and strength by the Grace of God they testified of the power of God manifested in Christ's resurrection.

God's Grace abounds to all the children of God. Romans 6:14 states that we are not under the law but under grace: Grace is the umbrella (covering) of the sons and daughters of God. John 1:16 further reveals, "And of His fullness we all have received (as many as received Him and His power to become the children of God), and grace for grace (grace multiplied). Grace is God's unlimited and unmerited favor toward sinners for their salvation.

Believers are to grow in the Grace of God. II Peter 3:8 exhorts us, "But grow in grace, and in the knowledge of our Lord and Savior Jesus Christ. To Him be glory both now and forever. Amen". We are to increase our knowledge of the Lord Jesus Christ and be complete (mature) in Him. We are His spiritual body and He is our Head: we are to know and understand all that Christ Jesus is to us and know what it means for us to be in Christ. II Timothy 2:15 instructs us, "Study (be diligent) to show (present) yourself approved unto God, a workman that needs not to be ashamed, rightly dividing the word of truth". We grow in grace by knowing and understanding all about the power of grace operative in our lives.

II Peter 1:2 greets us with these salutatory words, "Grace and peace be multiplied unto you through (in) the knowledge of God, and of Jesus our Lord". Finally, Hebrews 5:16 reveals to us His Throne of Grace, "Let us therefore come boldly (with confidence) unto the Throne of Grace, that we may obtain mercy, and find Grace to help in time of need".

CHAPTER FOURTEEN

GOD'S LOVE MANIFESTED IN HIS PEACE

PEACE ON EARTH, GOOD WILL TO MEN

When Jesus was born in Bethlehem of Mary, a multitude of an angelic host of heaven sang praises unto God saying, "Glory to God in the highest and on earth peace, good will toward men". Isaiah 9:6 reveals for our understanding, "For unto us a child is born, unto us a Son is given: and he government shall be upon His shoulder: and His Name shall be called Wonderful, Counselor, The mighty God, The everlasting Father, (and) The Prince of Peace".

This peace can only be fully realized worldwide when God sets up His Kingdom here on earth and He is established as our benevolent ruler bringing eternal peace to a riotous, greedy and sinful world. The world cries for peace and then institutes and endeavors to establish controls that can only breed warring factions. They cry peace, peace and then promote the violent overthrow of God's Kingdom here on earth, the Christian family of God; redeemed of the Lord. They scream peace but do all in their power to wipe away the name of the Prince of Peace, Jesus the Son of God. We have world organizations that are represented by representatives from all over the world and make great treaties and institute conditions and place sanctions, yet there is no peace. Greed, envy and the lust for power have caused the so called world peace keeping organization the United Nations to forfeit its original charter in favor of internal controlling factions who have done everything but keep the peace.

THE SOURCE OF OUR PEACE

Jesus said in John 14:27, "Peace I leave with you, My peace I give unto you: not as the world gives (peace), give I unto you. Let not your heart be troubled, neither let it be afraid". Our hearts will not be troubled, because Jesus lives in our hearts through the Holy Spirit of Truth. In verse 26 Jesus said He would send to us the Holy Spirit in His name to teach us all things concerning what Jesus said unto us. We are not of this world and there is within us the Spirit of God and of His Christ, Jesus. Philippians 4:7 proclaims, "And the Peace of God, which passes all understanding, shall keep (guard) your hearts and minds (in this world) through Christ Jesus". Galatians 5:22 also states that the fruit of the Spirit is love, joy, peace. Therefore, the source of our peace is our Triune God: God the Father, God the Son and God the Holy Spirit. They dwell within us, to preserve us blameless until the day of our redemption. I Thessalonians 5:23 Paul prays, "And the very God of peace sanctify you wholly (through and through); and I pray God your whole spirit and soul and body be preserved blameless (wholly consecrated to God) unto the coming of our Lord Jesus Christ".

GOD'S PEACE THROUGH THE ATONEMENT OF CHRIST

God so loves us that He gave to us Jesus as our Savior and loving Lord and our Prince of Peace. The world cannot know nor ever experience the Peace of God that passes all understanding. They cannot fathom it because peace is the nature of God. Jesus, our Peace provided it for us through His atonement. Isaiah 53:5 says, "But He (Jesus) was wounded (pierced through) for our transgressions, He was bruised (crushed) for our iniquities: the chastisement (needful to obtain for the wellbeing) of our peace was upon Him; and with His stripes we are healed". That is why Paul wrote to the Colossian Church, "And having made peace through the blood of His (Jesus) cross, by Him to reconcile all things unto Himself (God); by Him, I say, whether they be things in (on) earth, or things in heaven" (Colossians 1:20). His love purchased for us His peace, "In the body of His flesh through death, to present you holy and unblamable and unreprovable in His (God's) sight" (Colossians 1:21).

When we are justified (made righteous before God and secure) by faith, we have the peace that passes all understanding. Romans 5:1 affirms, "Therefore being justified by faith, we have peace with God through our Lord Jesus Christ". Isaiah 26:3 reiterates this truth, "You (God) will guard him and keep him in perfect and constant peace whose mind (both its inclination and its character) is stayed on (sustained by) You (God), because he commits himself to You, (trusts/have faith in God though

Jesus Christ), leans on You, and hopes confidently in You" (Amplified Bible).

OUR ADMONITION TO LIVE IN PEACE

II Corinthians 13:11b says to believers in Christ, "Be perfect (complete), be of good comfort, be of one mind (in Christ), live in peace; and the God of love and peace shall be with you". Our peaceful service of love to one another is given in Romans 12:18, "If it be possible, as much as lieth in (depends on) you, live peaceable with all men". A pure heart before God is dependent upon our pursuit of righteous behavior to, "Flee also youthful lusts: but follow righteousness, faith, love, peace, with them that call on the Lord out of a pure heart".

To live in peace also means that we practice peace in all of our relationships and as an instrument in the promotion of peace, a peacemaker. In His Beatitudes or Sermon on the Mount, Jesus proclaims to us, "Blessed are the peacemakers: for they shall be called the children (sons and daughters) of God" (Matthew 5:9). We are His offspring, progeny, and adopted heirs to inherit the Kingdom of God: like Father like son.

The Peace of our Prince of Peace edifies or builds us up in our faith in God. Romans 14:19 exhorts us, "Let us therefore follow after the things which make for peace and things wherewith one may edify another". I Peter 3:8-12 states that we are to be of one mind, compassionate toward one another, courteous, rendering blessings one to another. For if we would love and enjoy our life we would eschew (turn away from) evil and do good and "let him seek peace and ensue (pursue) it".

CHAPTER FIFTEEN

GOD'S LOVE MANIFESTED IN HIS JOY

THE JOY OF JESUS CROSS

As previously referred to Hebrews 12:2b reveals that, "for the joy that was set before Him" (Jesus) endured the cross despising the shame, has set down at the right hand of the throne of God". The word endured mirrors His steadfast, patient and fixed determination: His obedient response of love to the will of His Father God. The word despised means to think against or disregard to disesteem. Jesus thoughts were only on one thing; all other pain and suffering he endured due to His ordeal on the cross, although very real, was far below His one desire for which Jesus came to this earth. Jesus the Son of God became the Son of man: to suffer excruciating pain, to endure humiliation and shame and to gladly pour out the last drop of His precious blood and die that all of mankind may be reconciled back to God through His act of appeasement of the wrath of God against all sin.

All that Jesus endured and suffered on the cross cannot be compared to the Joy that was set (placed) before Him: seeing the fulfillment of God's (Triune God) plan for His children for time and eternity. It is the Joy that has echoed throughout the ages of time, since God created His most beloved of His creative fiat, man and woman. This God kind of Glory is the Divine Nature of Almighty God referred to as Joy unspeakable and full of glory; Glory that cannot be explained in finite or human terms, but only through the Eternal Spirit of Almighty God.

God's kind of love that gives of Himself for another being, God the Son even for those who were His enemies is without question unfathomable. Romans 5:7-8 explains to us, "For scarcely for a righteous man will one die: yet peradventure for a good man some would even dare to die. But God commended (demonstrated) His love toward us in that, while we were yet sinners (enemies of God), Christ died for us".

THE JOY OF OUR SALVATION

When I received Jesus as Lord and Savior there was a joy in my soul that made me to burst out in joyous song, "Glory Hallelujah"! For Jesus blood cleansed me and made me whole (spiritually complete in Christ Jesus). I was whole because I now had an oneness of purpose. I was whole because His divine power had revealed to me through His Spirit of Truth all things that pertain to life and godliness through the knowledge of Him Who called me to glory and virtue (II Peter 1:3).

When we are redeemed and seated around the Throne of God and singing joyous songs of praise and adoration unto Jesus Christ our Lord and Savior, the host of angels around the throne of God will have to fold their wings for they will not know nor can they share in the joy that our salvation brings. We will be before His Throne singing a new song, but I believe that it must be a rendition of Glory, Glory, Glory to Jesus Who was and is and has redeemed us by His Blood. Perhaps we will sing a new version of the Hallelujah Chorus that the Holy Spirit inspired Handel to produce in one night. To sing unto Jesus: King of Kings and Lord of Lords; King of Kings and Lord of Lords; Forever and ever, Forever and ever; Hallelujah! Hallelujah! Hallelujah! Amen!

When I first came to Jesus and met Him in my spirit man face to face, I knew that He had forgiven me of my sins and cleansed and washed me by His blood that He shed for me personally and personally for everyone who will receive Him as Savior and Lord. I knew because His Holy Spirit came to abide in the spirit and soul. At that time I was living at the YMCA in downtown South Bend, Indiana and I so hungered and thirsted to know more about Jesus and His love that I began to literally devour His Word, the Bible placed in my room by the Gideon's. I found His grace supplied my every need in life. As I studied and meditated upon His beatitudes; read His prayer to His and our Father in Heaven; the promise of His Holy Spirit that I had received; that He was the vine and I was the branch and in Him only I live and breathe and have my being; that He turns my sorrow to joy; that Jesus had already won for me the victory and overcome the world, the flesh and the devil; that Jesus prayed for me (John 17:1-26) and as my High Priest in heaven is still praying for me: I felt welling up within my heart a joy that is unspeakable and full of glory and I shouted, "Hallelujah, praise the Lord".

Oh, the half of what has been said and prepared for them that love Him has yet to be fully revealed.

I Corinthians 2:9-10 speaks to the heart and soul of all who have trusted Jesus as Lord, "But as it is written, 'Eye has not seen, nor ear heard, neither have entered into the heart of (unsaved) man, the things which God has prepared for them that love him'. But God has revealed them unto us (His elect) by His Spirit: for the Spirit searches all things, yea the deep things of God".

Oh, wonderful story of love; Holy Spirit reveal it to me over and over again. Oh, since that day, how I have hungered and thirsted to know all about Jesus; of His so great love; to know more about unseen things above; about Jesus and His glory; about His so great and wonderful salvation; about Jesus and how His Divine Power (the Power in His Blood) has given to us all things that pertain to life and godliness, through the knowledge of Him Who has called us to glory and virtue; about His exceeding great and precious promises that edifies us and increases my (our) faith and makes me (us) a partaker of His Divine Nature, escaping the corruption that is in the world through lust. Oh, truly, there is wonder working power in the blood of Jesus!

GOD'S JOY IS FULL AND FREE

When a vessel is full and continues to receive living waters its only recourse is to run over. God's joy, like His love runs over and splashes lavishly upon all those around the vessel. Psalm 23 says, "My cup runneth over". In other words, our vessel, our body, our spirit, and our soul when filled by the joy of the Lord who gives and gives and gives again; it must run over. This I believe is where the statement, "I am overjoyed" (running over with joy) comes from. Also to rejoice is to receive an abundance of joy; again and again and again. It comes from the presence of God through the presence of His Holy Spirit. Psalm 16:11 reveals that, "Thou (God) will show me the path of life: in Thy presence is fullness of joy; at thy right hand there are pleasures for evermore". In fact, one of the fruits of the Spirit is Joy. It follows in sequence after Love, the God kind of Love. Knowing that God never gives sparingly, but abundantly: good measure, pressed down, shaken together, overflowing He also gives to us His Joy (presence) evermore. He is Omnipresent.

His Joy is not only full in quantity but also full in quality as it comes from God. John 1:4 reveals that in Christ our joy is full, "And these things write we unto you, that your Joy may be full". Ephesians 3:19 states that we are, "To know the love of Christ, which passes knowledge, that you (we) might be filled with all the fullness of God". All the fullness of God is being filled with all of Him (God) and thereby manifest the attributes of His nature; the fruit of His Spirit: Love, Joy, Peace, Longsuffering, Gentleness, Goodness, Faithfulness, Meekness and self-control (Galatians 5:22).

Notice, it is the fruit (singular) of the Spirit. The Holy Spirit works within (spiritually energizes) us to grow in grace into the maturity of Jesus Christ our Lord. It is important that we have a listening ear to "hear what the Spirit says to your heart: (spirit/soul). Take time to read and mediate upon the Word of God, in the quietness far away from the maddening crowd so that you can hear what the Spirit says to you (us). Actually, Jesus said that the Holy Spirit, "Whom the Father will send in My (Jesus) name, He shall teach you all things, and bring all things to your remembrance, whatsoever I (Jesus) have said unto you" (John 14:26). Also, all that Jesus said to us as the Son of man is from the Father. Jesus said, "the Words that I speak unto you I speak not of Myself (my own authority): but the Father that dwells in me, He does the works" (John 14:10b). John 17:21 reveals that Jesus the Son is One with His Father God.

The unity of the Spirit within us is expressed in Ephesians 4:1-13 and in verses 12 and 13 Paul writes that the Holy Spirit within us fulfills all things in us, "For the perfection (growth in maturity) of the saints, for the work of the ministry, for the edifying of the body of Christ; Till (until) we all come in (into) the unity of the faith, and of the knowledge of the Son of God (Jesus, as the Son of man), into a perfect (mature) man (and woman), unto the measure of the stature of the fullness of Christ" John 15:11.

Jesus said in John 15:11, "These things I have spoken unto you, that My joy might remain in you, and that your joy might be full" and in John 16:24, "Hitherto have you asked nothing in my name: ask, and you shall receive, that your joy may be full". It is because we have received the knowledge of Him as the Son of God and as the Son of man as our salvation: "Behold, God is my salvation; I will trust, and not be afraid: for the Lord Jehovah is my strength and my song; He also is become my salvation. Therefore, with Joy shall you draw water out of the wells of salvation" (Isaiah 12:1-3). "But, whomsoever drinks of the water that I (Jesus) give him shall never thirst (again); but the water that I shall give him shall be in him a well (fountain) of water springing up into everlasting life" (John 4:14). Nehemiah 8:10 emphatically states, "The joy of the Lord is your (our) strength" (fortified place, rock, stronghold, fortress).

EVERLASTING JOY

As the redeemed of the Lord, our Joy is now in the present and forever in Eternity to come, Everlasting Joy. Isaiah wrote in Isaiah 51:11, "Therefore the redeemed of the Lord shall return, and come with singing unto Zion; and everlasting joy shall be upon their head (anointed with the joy of the Lord): they shall obtain gladness and joy; and sorrow and mourning shall flee away". It shall be upon our head because we are anointed with Joy (Psalm 23). God through Jesus Christ our Lord anoints our head with the oil of gladness, saturating our head with the oil of gladness; running down over our entire body. We have been anointed with the oil of gladness (Psalm 45:7). This is truly everlasting Joy because it is the Joy of the Lord and our Lord God is an Everlasting God.

David knew the Joy of the Lord in salvation, but because of His sin against God in his relationship with Bathsheba, he prayed, "Restore unto me the joy of Thy salvation; and uphold me with thy free (generous) Spirit". Today we can sing, "there is joy in my soul, oh, glory hallelujah" for Jesus blood makes me whole! For they that sow in tears (tears of humility and repentance) shall reap in joy (joy of salvation). The ransomed of the Lord shall sing songs of everlasting joy upon their heads and they shall obtain joy and gladness. Isaiah 65:14a proclaims, "Behold, My servants shall sing for joy of heart (for the deep feelings for God within my heart)".

Matthew 13:20 says that the Word is received with Joy by the believer and Luke 15:10 states that the entire host of heaven rejoices (there is joy in heaven) over one sinner that repents. That there is joy in heaven is evident throughout the word of God and it is everlastingly proclaimed for God is there. After John the Baptist saw and heard the voice of Jesus he said that His joy was fulfilled (John 3:29). In spite of all of the bonds and afflictions that Paul suffered, yet he testified that none of these things moved him for he did not count his life so dear, his only desire being that he might finish his course (as minister of the gospel of the grace of God in Christ Jesus) with joy (Acts 20:24).

The Greek language was used by God during this time because it was a most expressive language in the world for it could fully explain the full value or the meaning of what was said or felt. For example, the word love in the English is used to express different kinds of love. In the classical Greek language love for and of God is Agape, love for our brethren or friends is Philadelphia, love or desire for something is thelo, etc. Likewise the word joy in the Greek can be agalliasis, exultation gladness or exceeding joy (Jude 24, Luke 1:44, I Peter 4:13); Kauchaomai, joy as a boastful expression or glorying or rejoicing in something like ones accomplishments (Romans 5:11); chara, the word used most (90+ times more) which is exceeding joy, fullness of joy and complete joy.

In His love for us: God chose His perfect sacrifice to atone for our sins, Jesus His Son; the perfect language, Greek to express fully His love, mercy, and grace; His Holy Spirit as our comforter and guide for our revelation and edification; and His perfect plan of our so great salvation.

CHAPTER SIXTEEN

GOD'S LOVE DEMONSTRATED IN HIS JUDGMENT

JESUS LOVE AND JUDGMENT

John 5:22 reveals, "For the Father (Almighty God) judges no man (His created beings), but has committed all judgment unto the Son" (Jesus). This is because Jesus is the Son of God Who came to earth at the request (will) of His Father to be the Son of man and the atoning sacrifice for all the sins of mankind. Since Jesus is the one Who suffered; enduring the agonizing, tortuous, excruciatingly painful death upon the Cross of Calvary for mankind; Who freely gave his precious blood as a cleansing fountain open wide for all our (my) sin; Who died, despising the shame and humiliation of death on the cross; Who was raised for our justification (righteousness) and glorified, resuming His rightful place on His Throne on the right hand of God His Father; the King of Kings (of earth) and Lord of Lords (of earth) forever and ever. Anything and everything that pertains to His created beings, mankind is under the preeminence of Jesus Christ the Lord. He is Lord of all.

Colossians 1:14-22 reveals to us that Jesus is preeminent in the first creation of the Universe (all things were made by Him) and in His new creation: the Church (If any man be in Christ he is a new creation). He has been given preeminence over the Church as the Head of the Church. "In Whom (Jesus) we have redemption through His blood, even the forgiveness of sins: Who is the image of the invisible God, the first-born (creator) of every creature: For by Him were all things created, that are in heaven, and that are in (on) earth, visible, and invisible, whether they be thrones or dominions, or principalities (rulers), or powers (authorities): all things were created by Him, and For Him: And He is before all things, and by (in) Him all things consist (exist: operate effectively and held (cohered) efficiently together by His power). And He is the Head of the body, the Church: Who is the beginning, the first-born from the dead; that in all things He might have the pre-eminence. For it pleased the Father that in His Son Jesus should all fullness dwell;

And, having made peace through the blood of His cross, by Him to reconcile all things unto Himself; by Him, I say, whether they be things in (on) earth, or things in heaven. And you (we), that were sometime alienated and enemies in your mind by wicked works, yet now has He reconciled (restored in a favorable relationship with God) in the body of His flesh through death, to present you (us) holy and unblamable and unreprovable in His (God the Father's) sight". God sees us as washed, cleansed and sanctified through the blood of Jesus.

LOVE'S JUSTICE IN GOD'S JUDGMENT

In our own society, there had to be laws governing the affairs of mankind, otherwise everyone would do what they wanted to do against the desires of others and there would be chaos and anarchy. There had to be fair and equitable laws for society as a whole. From the beginning mankind realized that the Word of God was fair, equitable and righteous and touched every area of our life. Therefore, many democratic societies wrote constitutions that spelled out the basic governing policy of a nation. The Constitution of the United States of America was one such document that was based upon God's Word of Truth. The Preamble of that Constitution reads, "We the people of the United States of America, in order to form a more perfect union, establish justice, insure domestic tranquility, provide for the common defense, promote the general welfare, and secure the blessings of liberty to ourselves and our posterity, do ordain and establish this Constitution for the U. S. of America". Justice is God's primary method of governing His people and our Constitutional Justice is derived from His impartial, lawful and righteous omniscient Word of Truth.

Laws are made that reach into every area of our life; but in America it must conform to the primary rule of law written in the Constitution or it is unconstitutional; null and void. Supreme Court Justices are selected to guard against tyranny through unconstitutional laws and they together determine the legitimacy or constitutionality of the laws passed by Congress and signed by the President. Judgment is not only to condemn, convict and sentence, but also to pronounce justice, liberty and equity: a verdict of not guilty in conjunction with some equitable settlement. God's Judgment is saturated with His Love, His mercy, and

His Justice (Righteousness).

The first sentence of the second paragraph of the Declaration of Independence reads, "We hold these truths to be self-evident, that all men are created equal, that they are endowed by their Creator (God) with certain unalienable Rights that among these are Life, Liberty and the pursuit of Happiness". The Truth that our founding fathers wrote into their governing document, The Constitution of the United States of America is that which comes from the Word of God. This is apropos because Jesus is the Life, the Truth, the one who makes us Free Indeed and the Joy of our salvation.

Since our Lord God Almighty is Love and He manifests that love through His Son Jesus Christ the Lord as demonstrated through the power of His Holy Spirit of Truth; He is by His nature Just. The Justice of God is more than the finite human qualities associated with being just: fair, right, equitable, impartial, exact, accurate and precise. It also assumes the character of God in love, mercy, grace, lovingkindness, the God kind of impartiality, righteousness and His own personal benevolence. God cannot be anything other than what He is: Spirit, Love, Joy, Peace, Longsuffering, gentleness, goodness, faithfulness, meekness and control manifested through His own nature.

Why then, you may ask doesn't His created beings, mankind whom He so loves and for whom He has done everything in His power to justly provide for their every need, respond affirmatively to His love. God has created them and given them the breath of life; He created the earth as their habitat, the universe, the sun, moon and stars, the vegetation, the trees, the mountains majesty, the rivers, lakes, seas and oceans, wisdom, ability, willpower, strength, mental prowess, and the list could go on and on. Truly it is as stated in Acts 18:27, "for in Him (the Lord God Almighty) we live and move and have our being". To make sure that we have a right relationship with Him, our Lord God Almighty, He gave to us His son Jesus as the Son of man to suffer, bleed and die that we might have abundant life here and now and live in eternity with Him in His glory.

However, there came an iniquitous fly in the ointment of God's blessings, Satan, the father of all iniquity with his own concomitant coconspirators of; vice, wickedness, immorality, lawlessness, transgression of God's laws, criminal intent, hatred, malice, greed and an anti-God mentality. Satan was and is the original protagonist of God: the adversary (enemy) of God and of mankind. But remember, Satan was created an angel by God and not a human being: an angel of Light (Lucifer) to be God's director of the angelic host in the heavenly worship of the Lord God Almighty. Wanting to be ruler or prince of the earth and seeing that God had created mankind to be His chosen ones to populate and rule the earth, Satan became obsessed with His hatred for mankind and with subtle, deceiving predetermination connived to destroy his usurpers. Satan set out to destroy mankind through man's God given ability of willpower: the power to think, to reason, make decision and choose his own pathway to follow in life. Acting as an angel of light, a friend of mankind, he has successfully manipulated, deceived, and wantonly coerced mankind with the same kind of thinking that caused his impromptu, radical and sudden departure from the presence of God in heaven : to reject God and declare himself to be the CEO of the universe.

Therefore, God's love in judgment had to prevail, for the gates of hell cannot prevail against Truth and righteousness represented by the Lord God Almighty. God even loves his enemies, those who vociferously fight against His righteous cause. God has endeavored through the ministry of his sons and daughters who proclaim the Gospel message of Jesus Christ unto salvation to all the ages of time; to reconcile them back to God and restore them to their proper place in the economy (household management) of the Lord God Almighty. Ephesians 2:1-6 states that although those who walked previously according to the lustful behavior of this world, according to Satan's behest as children of disobedience, fulfilling the desires of our flesh and mind, and were by nature the children of wrath (judgment): God's mercy and love pursued them (us) until they (we) hungered and thirsted after His righteousness and reached out by faith and received Jesus Christ as Lord and Savior and became a new creation in Christ Jesus, for by His grace (benevolent favor) we are saved.

The righteousness of the law of God (law of the Spirit of life) which is by faith in Jesus Christ for all that believe, that God might redeem them that have sinned and come short of the glory of God. They are now justified freely (without effort or cost) by God's grace through redemption in His Son Christ Jesus, Who is the propitiation (substitute sacrifice) for our sin through faith in His blood, to declare His righteousness for the remission of (our) sins that are past, through the forbearance of God: to declare His righteousness that He (God) through Jesus Christ might be Just and the Justifier of him (those) who believe in Jesus as Lord and Savior (Romans 3:21-26).

MAN'S JUDGMENT IN DEFIANCE OF GOD'S LOVE

To begin with, mankind, all of humanity is imperfect because of their sin nature inherited through the sin of Adam and Eve their forbears in the Garden of Eden. Without becoming a new creation through faith in the blood of Jesus, mankind's judgment is polluted and self-serving. Even though we as a nation have a good Constitution based upon the just requirements of our Creator God, yet through the human element of selfish motives, lustful desires, greed and self-aggrandizement, mankind has deviously manipulated the laws of our land. Human judgment without the righteousness of God is often circumstantial, sometimes wrong, sometimes hasty and revengeful, full of conceit and prejudicial.

Truly humanity, without the guiding presence of God, armed with his God given intellect and willpower and tempted by the wiles of Satan, is prone to wander from the God of His first love and think of himself as the captain of his own soul while he endeavors to pull himself up by his own bootstraps. Mankind without his creator God is without God's armor of defense against the principalities, powers and the rulers of the darkness of this world. He who says, "No God for Me" soon finds himself in an eddying abyss of fluctuating desires that forcefully pulls them down and soon feels the need to cry out for someone, even God to help him. But every person is tempted when he is drawn away (from God) by his own lust (desires) and enticed (by Satan). Then when lust has conceived, it brings forth (gives birth to) sin: and when it (sin) is finished (full grown) it (always) brings forth death" (James 1:14-15).

God throughout His Holy Word and through His Holy Spirit of Truth is loudly proclaiming to all who will read and hear, "The wages of sin is death, but thanks be unto God Who through Jesus Christ His Son gives to us the victory that has already been won upon the Cross of Calvary". The Word plainly warns, "Be not deceived (By Satan and his anti-God world system); God is not mocked: for whatsoever man sows, that shall he also reap. For he that sows to his flesh shall of the flesh reap corruption; but he that sows to the Spirit shall of the Spirit reap life everlasting". In spite of all that mankind has used as a crutch, excuse, or to avoid culpability, God still says it like it is and warns every one of His created beings of the effects of sin and the dire significance of an eternity without God.

THE JUDGMENT SEAT OF CHRIST

Everyone born upon the face of this earth from Adam and Eve until the end of the age shall give an account to God. An indication of this judgment is given in Psalm 1:5, "Therefore the ungodly shall not stand in the judgment (judgment seat of Christ), nor sinners in the congregation of the righteous". II Corinthians 5:10 states, "For we (those in Christ Jesus) must all appear before the judgment set of Christ: that everyone may receive the things done in his body, according to that he has done, whether it be good or bad". This in the Greek is bema, an elevated place of judgment, a tribunal ascended by steps to where Christ is seated on the Throne. Although all of the children of God, His sons and daughters shall stand before Him and give account to him for all those things which we have done in the flesh and those things we have done in the Spirit, yet we are still the redeemed of the Lord and shall not stand in the Great White Throne Judgment to suffer the wrath of God, for we have been marked with the blood of Jesus as belonging to God. Tried in the fire of God's holiness, that which we have done for and in Christ shall be rewarded (built upon Christ's foundation; that which shines as gold, silver, precious stones), but those things that were of the flesh, for our own selves contrary to the will and way of God, shall be burned up whether it be considered by God to be wood, hay or stubble (straw).

I Corinthians 3:11-15 explains the judgment process of God for His saints, "For (no) other foundation can no man lay than that (which) is laid, which is Jesus Christ. Now if any man build upon this foundation (Jesus Christ as Lord and Savior) gold, silver, precious stones, wood, hay, stubble; Every man's work shall be made manifest (shown for what it is): for the day (day of the Judgment Seat of Christ) shall declare it, because it shall be revealed by fire; and the fire shall try every man's work of what sort it is". If any man's work abide (endures the test of fire), which he has built thereupon (Christ's foundation), he shall receive a reward. If any man's work shall be burned, he shall suffer loss (no reward): but he himself shall be saved; yet so as by (through) fire" (NKJV). Ephesians 2:10 states, "For we are His workmanship (creation), created in Christ Jesus unto (for) Good Works, which God has before ordained that we should walk in them"

I Corinthians 4:5 further explains, "Therefore judge nothing before the time, until the Lord comes, who both will bring to light the hidden things of darkness, and will make manifest (reveal) the counsels (motives) of the hearts. Then each one's praise will come from God". The parable of the talents emphasizes our personal preparedness and faithful service to Jesus Christ and the commendation and rewards of Christ at the Judgment Seat, "Well done, thou good and faithful servant: you have been faithful over a few things, I will make you ruler over many things: enter into the Joy of Your Lord".

THE GREAT WHITE THRONE JUDGMENT OF GOD

After the thousand years Millennial Reign of Christ that followed Armageddon, there will be a final judgment referred to as the Great White Throne Judgment of God. During the Millennial Reign of Christ, Jesus shall reign as King of Kings and Lord of Lords in righteousness, peace and love. During this time, Satan is bound for a thousand years after which he is given a little time (permission) to try (deceiving) the hearts of those born during this time. Some will be deceived and after this little sliver of time given to Satan, he will gather together his human dupes and his demons and devils of hell and make his final assault on earth against the saints of God and the Holy city of God. Fire is sent from God out of heaven to devour (overcome) them and their ambitions for the final time here on earth.

"And the devil that deceived them was cast into the lake of fire and brimstone, where the beast and false prophet are, and shall be tormented day and night for ever and ever. And I saw a great White Throne, and Him that sat on it, from whose face the earth and the heaven fled away; and there was found no place for them" (earth or heaven) (Revelation 20:11). The Great White Throne is situated in a place prepared for such an occasion by God. It is gloriously white and shinning, reflecting the purity, holiness and glory of God. This is the time of the second resurrection for those who will suffer the second death (eternal damnation) in the lake of fire, experienced only by the unsaved.

Revelation 20:12-15 continues with this scenario and reveals that the dead, great and small stand before God (Christ), "And the sea gave up her dead which were in it; and death and hell (hades) delivered up the dead which (who) were in them: and they were judged every man according to their works (wages of sin and death). And death and hell (hades-the temporary place until judgment day, of the bodies and souls of the lost-the unsaved) were cast into the lake of fire. This is the second death. And whosoever was not found written in the Book of Life was cast into the lake of fire".

Oh, my friends, those who read this writing, our life is as a vapor that soon vanishes away. What we do with the life God has so graciously given to us is very significant as to where we will spend eternity. Whether we are in Christ or without Christ will stand, will determine our final destination in the eternity to come. Those who are condemned by a loving God were condemned by their own choices in life: they loved darkness rather than light because their deeds were evil and they rejected the only hope they had; the only way to God; through the blood sacrifice of Jesus Christ the Lord. This is the unpardonable sin: to reject (blaspheme) the tender drawing appeal of the Holy Spirit to receive Jesus as Savior and Lord, because there is no other recourse to redemption and eternity with God: for there is no other name in heaven or on earth whereby we may be saved, only Jesus.

CHAPTER SEVENTEEN

KNOWING, SEEING AND EXPERIENCING THE LOVE OF GOD

KNOWING THE LOVE OF GOD

The love of God can only be known through Jesus Christ His Son for Jesus is God's gift of love to all mankind that they may be forgiven, cleansed, sanctified and reconciled as a member once again of the family of God. Made in God's image and receiving through the breath of God the spirit of Life within our inner most part we have become the children of God, having been born into the family of God. However, sin cancelled out the relationship and we became strangers, separated and alienated from God because of sin. Until Jesus came and shed His blood, died, was buried for our salvation and resurrected for our justification we were as dead in our trespasses and sins. We had become children of disobedience, fulfilling the desires of the flesh and of the mind and by nature the children of wrath.

But God so loved us that He would not let us go: He sent Jesus to be our substitute and bear the penalty for our sin, death. The innocent, pure Lamb of God shed His own blood and died for us that we may live in Him with God in the Eternity to come. Colossians 3:3 states, "For you are dead (died with Christ) and your life is hid with Christ in God".

I know that this is a repetition of what we have been saying throughout this writing, however, this truth must become ingrained (imbued, deep seated) within our being so that we may without question know His love for us.

The Holy Spirit is the one who brings all things to our attention concerning God. The Holy Spirit reveals to us the deep things of God and that includes His love for us. The Holy Spirit inspired the writing of the entire Word (logos) of God from Genesis to Revelation and throughout those pages of the Old and New Testaments (Covenants) of God we can know, feel and experience His Love. The Holy Spirit is a member of our One Triune God so that, it is Christ and God the Father also within us. This is a mystery to many; however, the Holy Spirit reveals to our spirit that although He abides within us and although He also represents the presence of God within us, yet, God the Father is on His Throne in Heaven as Jesus Christ our resurrected Lord and Savior is seated on His throne on God's right side. Jesus has become our High Priest so that we can come boldly to the Throne of Grace to receive help in time of need. We pray as instructed by Jesus, to God the Father (Our Father Who art in Heaven) through Jesus Christ as our High Priest, similar to that of the Old Testament Covenant without the inward presence of the Holy Spirit.

God is omnipresent; the Universe is filled with His glory. Christ is in us the Hope of Glory. That is why the Holy Spirit can be within the heart (spirit) and soul of everyone who receives Jesus as Lord and Savior. To finite mankind, this is impossible, but with God all things are possible.

When you think about How Great God is: How wonderful His works of Creation; How glorious His omnipotence, omniscience and Omnipresence; How supernatural His miraculous power of light, life and eternity; How perfect His ways and His manifestation of our salvation; How precious His Word of Power, His great and precious promises that can never be broken and His Holiness and Purity manifested in His Love for us! Whew! I have just scratched the surface of How Great our God is. And this Almighty God loves us! You and I!

Why wouldn't everyone want to know Him and about His love for us?

SEEING THE LOVE OF GOD

We live by faith, not by sight. However, within our heart of faith we see Jesus as the Way, the Truth and the Life. We see with the eye of our spirit man energized by the Holy Spirit, the things of God that by faith we hope to attain and obtain. According to Hebrews 11:1, Now, (in the present) faith is the assurance (the confirmation, the title deed) of things (we) hope for, being the proof of things (we) do not see and the conviction of their reality (faith perceiving as real fact what is not revealed to the senses)" (Amplified Bible). Therefore, faith is not seeing with the natural eye, but perceives (sees and understands) with the spiritual eye by which we are assured and convinced that what we have hoped for (the blueprint of our faith) is substance (real) and our evidence is that our faith has touched the realm of faith through the Spirit of God.

As previously explained in this writing, the inward man is the spirit man and as a child of God we have abiding within our spirit man the Holy Spirit to lead and guide us into all truth. The Holy Spirit provides the energy (dunamis-power) to see with our spiritual eye of faith. Job, a man of faith suffering a painful ordeal in his life affirmed his faith when he said, "For I know that my Redeemer liveth, and that He shall stand at the latter day upon the earth: And though after my skin worms destroy this body, yet in my flesh shall I see God: Whom I shall see for myself and my eyes shall behold, and not another (stranger); though my reins be consumed (how my heart yearns) within me" (Job 19:25-27). The Amplified Bible says, "And after my skin, even this body, has been destroyed, then from my flesh or without it I shall see God". Again, I Corinthians 2:9 reveals, "But as it is written, eye (physical eye) has not seen, nor ear heard, neither has entered into the heart (spirit) of man, the things which God has prepared for them that love Him. But God has revealed them unto us by His Spirit: for the Spirit searches all things, yea, the deep things of God. For what man knows the things of a man, save (except) the spirit of man which is in him? Even so the things of God knows no man, but the Spirit of God".

Faith believes: that all things are possible with God; that Jesus reveals Himself in a very real sense; that what God has said is true, fixed and eternal; that He is able to do above and beyond whatever we can ask or think. Faith receives all that the benevolent hand of God supplies: life; healing; provision; protection; God's Covenant promises; Salvation; forgiveness; cleansing; adoption into the family of God; sanctification; edification; inheritance of eternal life with God; and God's faithfulness to us according to His Word of faith. Faith loves: faith operates by love; faith responds affirmatively to love; faith reaches out and embraces others with God's love; faith actively engages (is active) in demonstrating love for God and our neighbors.

EXPERIENCING THE LOVE OF GOD

Love is not stagnate, but is active and alive. Love needs to pour itself out, to reach out, and to find someone upon who love can reveal itself in active participation. Love needs to be experienced, that is why God commanded us to, "you shall love the Lord your God with all your heart (spirit), and with all your soul, and with all your strength, and with all your mind; and your neighbor as yourself". Love needs to manifest itself actively by giving and giving and giving again. Love does not depend upon the reciprocity of others, but gives: it is its nature.

God is Love for he actively sought us: even when we were enemies; when we, his created beings turned our backs on Him; by providing for us full and free salvation; by giving to us His Holy Spirit to abide within us, comfort us, guide us, and lead us into an eternal love relationship with Himself.

We experience the Love of God when we seek Him, receive Him as Almighty God, love Him, know Him through Jesus Christ our Savior and Lord, serve Him as ministers of the Gospel of Jesus Christ, and be like Him, until He becomes our all and all. The experience of the Love God involves our entire person: spirit, soul and body. We experienced the Love of God when we become partakers of His Divine Nature by believing and receiving the knowledge of Him through His exceeding great and precious promises.

We experience God's Love at the Cross of Calvary. For love was placed on the cross, freely gave of His blood, was buried, but triumphantly rose again, a victor over Satan, death, hell and the grave. God's Love through Jesus Christ demonstrated to all mankind that it is stronger than any of the enemies of the spirit, soul or body. God's love is truly penetrating, all-encompassing and contagious.

To fully abide in His Love we must answer the questions posed by Elisha A. Hoffman, "Is Your All on the Altar?" In this song he writes, "You have longed for sweet peace, and for faith to increase, and have earnestly, fervently prayed; but you cannot have rest or be perfectly blest, until all on the altar is laid. Would you walk with the Lord, in the light of His Word, and have peace and contentment always? You must do His sweet will; to be free from all ill, on the altar your all you must lay. Oh, we never can know what the Lord will bestow of the blessings for which we have prayed. Until our body and soul, He does fully control, and our all on the altar is laid. Who can tell all the love He will send from above, and how happy our hearts will be made; of the fellowship sweet we shall share at His feet, When our all on the altar is laid." Then the chorus asks and proclaims, "Is our all on the altar of sacrifice laid? Your heart, does the Spirit control? You can only be blest and have peace and sweet rest as you yield Him your body and soul".

CHAPTER EIGHTEEN

GREATEST OF THESE IS LOVE

OUR RESPONSE TO THE LOVE OF GOD

In the great Love Chapter, I Corinthians 13:13 the Word of God explicitly reveals, "And now abideth faith, hope and charity, these three, but the greatest of these is charity (love)". Many times well-meaning children of God go on their own quest in grasping at legitimate concerns as recorded in the Word of God but forget Who Jesus is, What He said and Why He came to earth to become the Son of Man since He is the Son of God. They take the Word of God and without any consideration of the whole of God's plan of Salvation twist it into a tradition of man, not in keeping with God's commandment of Love and Mercy toward all mankind, especially our brothers and sisters of the household of faith. Galatians 6:10 says, "As we have therefore opportunity, let us do good unto all men, especially unto them who are of the household of faith".

FOR GOD SO LOVED

John 3:16-17 emphatically reveals God's plan. It was for Jesus to come and suffer, bleed and die so that we may be forgiven of our sins and reconciled to God. Jesus came not to condemn man, because, since the fiasco of the Garden of Eden man was already in a state of condemnation. "For God so loved the world that He gave His only begotten Son, that whosoever believeth in Him should not perish, but have everlasting life. For God sent not His Son into the world to condemn the world; but that the world through Him might be saved". Jesus demonstrated this fact when He was tempted by the Pharisees to condemn a woman caught in the act of adultery, an act punishable by death (stoning), not because of the act she had committed in breaking the law, but they wanted to accuse Jesus because they knew of His forgiving mercy. Jesus said unto them, "He that is without sin among you, let Him (or her) first cast a stone at her". One by one the accusing assembly threw down their stones and left the scene before them. Jesus then spoke to the adulteress and asked, "Woman, where are those accusers? Hath no man condemned thee?" The woman answered Jesus that no man stayed to condemn her and Jesus said unto her, "Neither do I condemn thee, go, and sin no more".

Jesus wants us to keep His commandments in Love, not in condemnation. There is not one of God's children that has not sinned at one time or another. We are to strive to walk in the Spirit and not fulfill the lusts of the flesh, but, the major attributes of God through Jesus Christ His Son is mercy, grace and love. In Matthew 22:34-40 Jesus is confronted by the religious Pharisees and tempted with the question concerning the great commandment of the law to which Jesus answered, "Thou shalt love the Lord thy God with all thy heart, and with all thy soul, and with all thy mind. This is the first and great commandment. And the second is like unto it, Thou shalt love thy neighbor as thyself". Colossians 3:14 exhorts us, "And above all these things (numerated Christian virtues) put on charity (love), which is the bond of perfectness". God is Love and we are to be His Sons and Daughters of Love not condemnation. We were never given the apostleship or discipleship of judgment, God through Jesus Christ is our only Judge. We are not to judge things before time, for Jesus will Judge on that Day.

JUDGE NOT THAT YE BE NOT JUDGED

Matthew 7:1-5 exposes our judgmental attitudes under the guise of religiosity, "Judge not, that ye be not judged. For with what judgment ye judge, ye shall be judged: and with what measure ye mete (use to judge by), it shall be measured to you again. And why beholdest thou the mote (speck) that is thine brother's eye, but considereth the beam (plank) that is in thine own eye? Or how wilt thou say unto thy brother, Let me pull out the mote out of thine eye; and behold, a beam is in thine own eye? Thou hypocrite, first cast out the beam out of thine own eye; and then shalt thou see clearly to cast out the mote out of thy brother's eye". I John 1:8-9 states, 'If we say we have no sin, we deceive ourselves, and the truth is not in us. If we confess our sins, He is faithful and just to forgive us our sins, and to cleanse us from all unrighteousness".

Our sins also include usurping God's prerogative to Judge His own servants. The ministers of the Gospel of Jesus Christ preach the Gospel of Salvation through Jesus Christ the Lord in revelation of sins and lawless living and also in not being a light of the world, but NOT a judge of our brethren in Christ. Romans 3:23 states, "For all have sinned and come short of the glory of God; Being justified freely (without any cost) by His grace through the redemption that is in Christ Jesus". We preach and teach from the foundation of Jesus Christ the Lord, Love not condemnation and thereby help others to seek Jesus, He only is the one that can forgive and restore. Who are we that we with audacity judge another man's servant? God said, "All souls are mine" and He therefore is the judge of all of His creation. Satan is so sly and wily that if we are not careful we will fall into his trap of being religiously judgmental. Many Christians confuse their indignation of the sins of others and not by the Word, "All scripture is given by inspiration of God, and is profitable for doctrine, for reproof, for correction, for instruction in righteousness: That the man (or woman) of God may be perfect, thoroughly furnished unto all good works" (II Timothy 3:16-17).

THE PRIDE OF LIFE (HAUGHTY SPIRIT)

Mathew 23:23-25 makes this condemnation of Pharisaical pride, "Woe unto you Scribes, and Pharisees, hypocrites! For ye pay tithes of mint and anise (out of a heart of boastful pride pay tithes of the smallest detail), and have omitted (neglected) the weightier matters of the law, Judgment (Justice), mercy, and faith: these ought ye to have done, and not to leave the other undone. Ye blind guides, which strain at a gnat, and swallow a camel (you accuse your brethren of a fault and thereby display your own abominable carnal conduct). Woe unto you, scribes and Pharisees, hypocrites! For ye make clean the outside of the cup and of the platter, but within they are full of extortion and excess" (your heart is not right toward God).

Jesus said in I John 3:23-24, "And this is the commandment, That we should believe on the name of His Son Jesus Christ, and love (with the God kind of love) one another, as He gave us commandment. And he that keepeth His commandments dwelleth in Him (Jesus). And hereby we know that He abideth in us by the Spirit which He hath given us".

The first fruit of life of the Holy Spirit of God and of Christ Jesus is love, followed by joy, peace, longsuffering (patience), gentleness, goodness, faithfulness, meekness and self-control (temperance). I fail to see a proud or indignant heart (spirit) as a fruit of the Spirit.

Another example of how God looks at our conduct before Him in Love is found in His parable of the unforgiving servant found in Matthew 18:23-35. Here Jesus taught His disciples saying that in His Kingdom of Heaven there was a king who audited (balanced the books of righteousness?) and found that one servant owed Him a huge debt (that he himself could not repay) and commanded him, his wife and children and all that he had to be put in prison until the debt was paid. But the servant fell down on his knees and prostrated himself before the king and begged forgiveness and patience and vowed that he would pay all that he owed. The king was moved with compassion and loosed him and forgave him his debt that he owed. That same servant went out and found one of his servants that owed him a very small debt, and with vindictiveness demanded that he pay all that he owed. The indebted servant likewise fell down on his knees and begged for mercy but he would not and cast him into prison. When the news of this travesty of justice came to the kings attention he sent for the servant whom he had forgiven and said, "O thou wicked servant, I forgave thee all that debt, because thou desiredst (begged) me; Shouldest not thou also have had compassion on thy fellow servant, even as I had on thee? ". The servant then was cast into prison until he paid all his debt. Some Christians are in their righteous zeal misled by their own exalted position of guiltlessness (I am so good, don't you wish you were).

ONLY THE BLOOD OF JESUS

The blood of Jesus Christ our Lord cleanseth us from all sin (I John 1:7). All means all. There is no sin or spot that the blood of Jesus cannot cleanse. The word cleanse used here means to completely blot out so that there is no indication that there ever was a spot or sin. And the Word tells us that when we are cleansed we are set free and whom the Son has set free is free indeed (John 8:36). No more guilt, no more condemnation, cleansed and made pure. There are those who continually pursue strife by digging up the dead things that are buried as a testimony against God's children of dust. He (God) knoweth our frame. Jesus said, "Let the dead bury the dead". The blood will also cleanse that person from sinful pride if they will repent and keep his commandment of loving one another.

STRIFE AMONGST THE BRETHREN – WHICH GOD HATES MOST

The Word of God reveals in Proverbs 6:16-19, "These six things doth the Lord hate; yea, seven are an abomination unto Him (Jesus): A proud look (haughty eyes), a lying tongue and hands that shed innocent blood, A heart that deviseth wicked imaginations (devises wicked plans), feet that be swift in running to mischief (evil works), and he that sows discord among brethren (strife)". Some so called Christians are so eager to show their zeal for the Lord that they go before Him and heed not His admonition of Love and Mercy and blab out the wretchedness of another brother or sister all in the name of being a saint of God when in actuality they are the courier of the devil. You are a Pharisee. I Corinthians 3:3 further states, "For ye are yet carnal whereas there is among you envying, and strife and divisions (dissensions) are ye not carnal, and walk as men (of this world)?" Galatians 5:19 further explains, "Now the works of the flesh are manifest (evident), which are these; adultery, fornication, uncleanness, lasciviousness, Idolatry witchcraft (drugs used in sorcery), hatred, variance (contentions), emulations (jealousies), wrath, strife (selfish and prideful ambitions contrary to the will of God), seditions, heresies, envying's, murders, drunkenness, revellings, and such like of the which I tell you before, as I have also told you tin time past, that they which do such things shall not inherit the kingdom of God". Paul nails this abomination of many proud and haughty so called Christians, "Because the carnal mind is enmity (enemy) against God; for it is not subject to the law (or will) of God, neither indeed can be. So then they that are of the flesh (not of the Spirit) cannot please God" (Romans 8:7-8).

In Matthew 18:21 Peter asks the Lord Jesus how often shall I forgive my brother of his trespasses against me? Recorded in the next verse Jesus answered, "I say not unto thee, until seven times; but, until seventy times seven". Unlimited forgiveness characterizes the demeanor of a true disciple of Christ. Jesus Himself our example said, "If we (you and

I) confess our sins, He (Jesus) is faithful and just to forgive us our sins, and to cleanse us from all unrighteousness". All sins can be and are forgiven, for all sin is ultimately against God. David said in his prayer for forgiveness of his sins of adultery with Bathsheba and murdering her husband Uriah, "Against Thee (God) and Thee only, have I sinned, and done this evil in thy sight" (Psalm 51:4a).

We are a glorious church without spot or wrinkle (Ephesians e5:27). One of the wrinkles that may be present in the body of Christ is strife. Again, in Galatians 5:14-15 explains to us the children of God of our behavior of one to another. "For all the law is fulfilled in one word, even in this: Thou shalt love thy neighbor as thyself. But if ye bite and devour one another, take heed that ye be (are) not consumed one of another". Previously in verse 9 we read, "A little leaven leavens the whole lump" (a little false doctrine permeates, corrupts the whole lump, the church). Proverbs 10:12 rightly admonishes us, "Hatred stirs up strife's; but love covers all sins.

JEWISH AND CHRISTIAN HYPOCRITES

Matthew 23:15 records these words of Jesus to the hypocritical religious Pharisees of His day, "Woe unto you, scribes and Pharisees, hypocrites! For ye compass (travel) sea and land to make one proselyte (convert by your good deeds), and when he is made (a convert), ye make him twofold more the child of hell (Gehenna) than yourselves". Pride always goeth before a fall and that disciple who with presumptuous pride walked around with a haughty spirit and a proud look will not receive anything of the Lord except in answer to a prayer of forgiveness and reconciliation. Philippians 2:3 exhorts us as brothers and sisters in Christ, "Let nothing be done through strife or vainglory; but in lowliness of mind let each esteem (the) other better than themselves".

PRAYERFULLY STUDY, SEARCH OUT AND MEDITATE ON HIS WORD OF TRUTH

II Timothy 2:15 admonishes us to, "Study to show thyself approved unto God, a workman that needeth not to be ashamed, rightly dividing the

Word of Truth". The word study is best interpreted in this same verse of scripture according to the Amplified Bible, "Study and be eager (zealously earnest) and do your utmost to present yourself to God approved (tested by trial), a workman who has no cause to be ashamed, correctly analyzing and accurately dividing (rightly handling and skillfully teaching) the Word of Truth. The many different denominations and sects with varying opinions concerning the Word of God happen when one does not sufficiently search the Word of God for His Word of Truth. They take a pet scripture verse and complicate the matter and compound the error by aligning it with other passages of scripture that are not compatible with one another. They fail to see that it is important to make an extinction and to know who is speaking and to whom – the church or Jewish people. It is important that they keep all verses of scripture in context for the Word of God is a true and faithful witness of itself. God can swear by no other Supreme Truth than Himself. An extension of His oath is through His Holy Spirit of Truth and The Word of Truth, His Son Jesus (Hebrews 6:13.

To rightly divide the Word of Truth we must first be a child (Son or Daughter) of God because it is His (our Fathers) Word. We must have the indwelling presence of His Holy Spirit of Truth because it is the Holy Spirit of Truth that reveals God's Word to us. II Corinthians 2:9-11 explains this truth to us, "But it is written, 'Eye hath not seen, nor ear heard, neither have entered into the heart of man, the things which God hath prepared for them that Love Him'. But God hath revealed them unto us (His legitimate Sons and Daughters) by His Spirit: for the Spirit searches all things, yea, the deep things of God. For what man knoweth the things of a man, save the spirit of man which is in him? Even so the things of God knoweth no man, but the Spirit of God". The phrase unto us emphasizes the wonderful privilege that we have as His children to be recipients of the hidden mystery by the Divine Revelation of His Word of Truth.

God's Word is easy to read and to understand what saith the Lord God Almighty on everything that pertains to life and godliness. James 3:17 explains, "But the Wisdom that is from above (from God) is first pure, then peaceable, gentle, and easy to be entreated, full of mercy and good fruits, without partiality, and without hypocrisy". The Word used here for entreated in the Greek means to perfect or complete in persuading what thus sayeth the Lord God. I Peter1:3 states, "According as His (God's) Divine Power hath given unto us all things that pertain unto life and godliness, through the knowledge of Him that hath called us to glory and virtue". God has given to every man created or born into this world a measure of faith sufficient to receive His Word of Truth. God has given to all those who desire to know Him and to seek Him (through Jesus Christ His Son) and receive Jesus Christ as Lord and Savior the privilege of becoming an intimate part of His Family, the Family of God as adopted Sons and Daughters of the Most High God and brother s and sisters of Jesus Christ His Son. In fact we become joint heirs to the unsearchable riches of God in Christ Jesus our Lord.

THE ERROR OF MAN'S WISDOM IN INTERPRETING THE WORD OF GOD

The reason so many err in interpreting the Word of God is that they do not know God and or they have preconceived ideas of what is Truth. They jump out into the deep before they know and understand first the power of God unto Salvation or as a child of God they do not let the Holy Spirit lead them into all areas of Truth. Recorded in John 16: 13-15 Jesus reveals to us, "Howbeit when He, the Spirit of Truth, is come, He will guide you into all truth; for He shall not speak of Himself, but whatsoever He shall hear (from the Father and I), that shall He speak: and He will show you things to come. He shall glorify Me for He shall receive of mine (that which is of Christ) and shall show it unto you. All things that the Father hath are mine: therefore said I that He shall take (have) of mine, and shall show it unto you".

This verse of scripture tells us that the Holy Spirit of Truth will lead us into all Truth which He has received from God the Father through Jesus Christ the Son. Anyone who receives information from another must consider three important areas of concern. He must know who is speaking, what is being said and from whose point of view. Jesus came to earth as the Son of man to begin His ministry with God's original elect, the Jews. His disciples since the beginning of the Church spoke those things that Jesus wants revealed to the church, His other elect. Both will be grafted together as one Family of God in Christ Jesus in the millennium to come.

DIVORCE UNDER THE MOSAIC LAW AND LOVE UNDER GRACE

If you want light on any subject, let's say divorce (a very controversial subject today) then you would go to the Word and search out the meaning in the light of the Mosaic Law and in the teachings of Christianity. One applies to the Law given to the Hebrew elect of God and the other was given under the Law of Love to the Church by Jesus Christ the Lord. Certainly in the beginning God's plan for Adam and Eve and future generations was that since Eve is bone of Adams bone and flesh of Adams flesh the two become one. In a family situation, a man (husband) would leave his mother and father and cleave to his wife (Genesis 2:22-24). God never intended for a married man and woman to raise children unto God and then with selfish motives divorce one another for another spouse.

Jesus was asked by the Pharisees (Jews) the question, "Is it lawful for a man to put away his wife? Tempting him". Jesus answered, "What did Moses command you (under the law)?" And they said that Moses let them write a bill of divorcement (to get a divorce). Jesus answer was in response to a Hebrew under the doctrine of Mosaic Law. "For the hardness of your (Jews) heart he (Moses) wrote this precept. But from the beginning of the creation God made them male and female. For this cause shall a man leave his father and mother, and cleave to his wife; and they twain (the two of them) shall be one flesh: so they are no more twain, but one flesh. What therefore God hath joined together, let not man put asunder". Later his disciples asked Jesus the same question and Jesus answered as a Jewish Rabbi, "Whosoever shall put away his wife, and marry another, committeth adultery against her. And if a woman shall put away her husband, and be married to another, she committeth adultery" (Mark 10:2-12).

In the Sermon on the Mount Jesus was speaking to a Jewish congregation when He said, "Think not that I am come to destroy the law, or the prophets; I am not come to destroy, but to fulfill" (Matthew 5:17). Romans 13:8 reveal that, "For all the law is fulfilled in one word, even in this; 'Thou shalt love thy neighbor as thyself'". Again, Romans 13:8 states, "Owe no man anything, but to love one another: for he that loves another hath fulfilled the law". As recorded in Matthew 22:40 Jesus speaks of loving God with all of the heart, soul and mind and our neighbor as ourselves and then says, "On these two commandments hang all the law and the prophets". Love is the greatest of all the law and commandments. It supersedes any law or commandment in that all sin or lawlessness against God (the breaking of his Law or commandment) is by petition or request, forgiven, period!

On adultery when He said, "Ye have heard that it was said, by them of old time, 'Thou shalt not commit adultery: But I say unto you, that whosoever looks on a woman to lust after her hath committed adultery with her already in his heart" (Matthew 5:27-28). But, remember only God can judge His own servants whether Jews or the Church. This is a personal matter between God and His elect whether it is under the Mosaic Law for the Jews or under the commandment of love for the church. As Christians under the Law of Love we are to discern between good and evil through His Word of Truth rightly divided, and separate ourselves from the evil of this world, however, we do not judge others, only their sin and we love them through Christ who first loved us. We do not hate them, we only abhor the sin, but we love them. Newly saved couples from divorce situations need God's love manifested through the Christian Church, not ridicule and strife. Genuine confession of their sin to God is between them and God through the sacrifice of His Jesus Christ Who is the Lord of all things. Their testimony and confession of faith cleanses them from all sin. God has given Jesus preeminence over all things that pertain to individual members of the church and stirring up strife among the brethren is an abomination unto God. Proverbs 6:16-19 lists seven deadly sins that are an abomination unto God and the seventh God list as he one He hates most, "he that soweth discord (strife) among the brethren".

Then on divorce Jesus said to the Jews, "It hath been said, 'whosoever shall put away his wife, let him first give her a writing of divorcement: But I say unto you, That whosoever shall put away his wife, saving for the cause of fornication, causes her to commit adultery: and whosoever shall marry her that is divorced committeth adultery'" (Matthew 5:31-32). As Christians, we are not to involve ourselves in adultery or fornication whether it occurred before or after our conversion, but when one of God's own with an honest heart come before Him in repentance (for their sin which was against their own bodies, our children and our spouses) He (Jesus) forgives them and cleanses us from all unrighteousness (I John 1:9). Read the entire 51st Psalm where David prays for cleansing of His Sin under the Mosaic Law. He prostrates himself upon the mercy and loving kindness and tender mercies of God and acknowledges that, "Against Thee (God), Thee only, have I sinned, and done this evil in thy sight: that Thou mightiest be justified (be found Just) when thou speaks, and be clear (blameless) when Thou judges".

Why do so many take the sins of others personally when all sin is perpetrated against God. Our sin truly will affect others (which is what sin ultimately does) as when David committed adultery with Bathsheba which resulted in the death of Uriah her husband (to cover up David's adulterous act). Although a baby was conceived, born and died because of David's sin, however, the next child born to David and Bathsheba was not to blame for their previous adulterous act and God raised Solomon up to be a great leader of His people.

WORLDLY LUST SUFFOCATES GOD'S LOVE

The second paragraph of our Declaration of Independence emphatically declares, "We hold these truths to be self-evident, that all men are created equal, that they are endowed by their Creator with certain unalienable Rights that among them are Life, Liberty and the pursuit of Happiness. That to secure these rights, Governments are instituted among Men, deriving their just Powers from the consent of the governed, --That whenever any Form of Government becomes destructive of these ends, it is the Right of the People, to alter or to abolish it, and to institute a new Government, laying its foundation on such principles and organizing powers in such form, as to them shall seem most likely to affect their Safety and Happiness".

The great sin of America today is abortion. The killing (murder) of innocent babies who had nothing to do with the sin of their parents is an abomination unto God. Evil men without conscience have made and passed laws to take the life of the innocent babies, the precious progeny of our nation and judged these laws to be just under the guise of freedom of choice of the mother. It does not consider the desires of the father even though both were engaged in lustful activities and even though part of the father (his seed) together with the woman (her body) produced the innocent lovable child. The argument that the woman carries the baby in her body and rightly so, because God created them to be mothers. This does not give them the right to kill the innocent baby. When a woman and a man consent together to have illicit or even legal sex under the law, all right concerning the wellbeing of the child rests with both.

But abortion has fostered a plan of parenthood where they have eliminated the first cause of being a parent, the child. It has enlisted the ranks of greedy men and women (doctors and nurses – a misnomer) who have made fortunes in their perverted chosen profession. Their greed eventually has turned into murderous evil desire to extinguish a precious life under the pretense that it is a legitimate profession. Such murderous activities were once banned and the laws of our land had stiff penalties for those unscrupulous doctors and nurses and their cohorts who plied their art of butcherly carving up of little lovable innocent babies, whose cries for help and justice were muffled by their cruel hands. Actually, the new laws of pro-choice is one sided and not equal for it takes away the rights and denies the freedom of the unborn whose hearts are stilled by the cruel instruments of pain and suffering and annihilated by an unmerciful court of human justice (a misnomer). With every beat of their heart they cry out for nature's gift of life soon to be denied. Every heartbeat of every aborted child cries out frantically for help from the tribunal of justice of our highest court, but there is none to hear for the court is too busy giving their self-righteous approval to an act that is an abomination to the Judge of the Universe, Almighty God.

I implore you! I beseech you! Listen to the whimpering voices of these precious souls from all races of humanity. Hear their tearful cries as the scalpel in the hands of a fiend carves deep to do its bloody work. Yes this is a vivid picture of a life, an unborn infant, a created being of God ending prematurely by permission of our court system But this brief description does not even begin to tell the whole story of the excruciating pain and extreme suffering endured as their precious bodies are mutilated or their brains sucked out and thrown in the trash heap or, God forbid, used for experimental purposes. Hitler and his Nazi murdering henchmen could take a lesson from the page of the new Hippocratic Oath (oath of hypocrisy) of our sophisticated doctors in America today. Doesn't our Pledge of Allegiance to the Flag (in essence America) say, "With liberty and justice for all?" It took America a long time to rightly acknowledge a previously unprotected people of America who had their rights taken away far too long, until the enforcement of the Fourteenth Amendment. It took men like Abraham Lincoln and Dr. Martin Luther King to right such an injustice to a segment of our free society. Let me say this, search it out for yourselves that neither of these two great men of our American heritage would have condoned such practices.

Is there anyone of prominence in America today that will stand up for the unborn whose beating heart cries out for a chance to experience America's promise to them: life, liberty and the pursuit of happiness and save them from the acts of tyranny? Are we going to have another century pass before we acknowledge and protect another unprotected part of our society, the unborn child? What part of, "With liberty and justice for all" do our congressmen, judges and president not understand? Think about that!! There can be no argument that a heart beating within the breast of an unborn child is no less alive than that of a child just born. Murder is the taking of a life without cause and there is no cause that justifies murder by abortion!

LOVE IS THE PASSION OF THE WISDOM OF GOD

Concerning the commandment of the Lord that we should let the mind of Christ be in us and rule our conduct, especially toward the household of God, it is evident by the word of God that the mind of Christ was, "That we should believe on the Name of His (God's) Son Jesus Christ, and love one another, as He gave us commandment" (I John 3:28). James further asks and then explains, "Who is a wise man endued (has understanding) with knowledge among you? Let him show out of a good conversation (conduct of life) that his works (that his works are done in the) meekness of wisdom. But if ye have bitter envying and strife in your hearts, glory not (do not boast), and lie not against the truth. This wisdom descended not from above, but is earthly, sensual, (and) devilish. For where envying and strife is, there is confusion and every evil work. But the wisdom that is from above is first pure, then peaceable, gentle, and easy to be entreated, full of mercy and good fruits, without partiality, and without hypocrisy. And the fruit of righteousness is sown peace of them that make peace. Jesus didn't cast the woman caught in adultery out with vindictiveness but with a loving heart He (Jesus) forgave her of her sin and cleansed her from all unrighteousness. Woe unto them that take their brother or sister by the throat and with righteous indignation (self-pronounced righteousness) casting them out of their midst as if they were doing God a favor. They are the ones that stand in judgment! If it is the sin of divorce or adultery that you abhor, remember God can forgive all sins and cleanse from all unrighteousness (I John 1:9). God in speaking to all His children said to us in I John 1:8, "If we say that we have no sin, we deceive ourselves, and the truth is not in us" (I John 1:8). So you see be careful when you condemn others that justice is not meted out to you also in like judgment. Hate the sin but love the sinner!

THE PARABLE OF THE SELF RIGHTEOUS AND THE SINNER

A careful student of the Word of God would know that self-righteousness is a sin even as adultery or lying. The Word says, "All have sinned and come shot of the glory of God" (what God demands of His children) Romans 3:23. Sin is sin regardless of the cloak it wears and we are all without excuse. However, the grace of God through the shed blood of Jesus His Son cleanseth us from all sin. A child of God is to live in Love and Harmony with those who rightfully confess Jesus as Lord and Savior and have received cleansing from all their sins. In the Parable of the Pharisee (self-righteous religious leader) and the Publican (sinful tax-collector) Jesus relates this example, "The Pharisee stood and prayed thus with himself, 'God, I thank thee that I am not as other men are, extortionist, unjust, adulterers, or even as this publican. I fast twice in a week, I give tithes of all that I possess'. And the publican standing afar off would not lift up so much as his eyes unto heaven, but smote upon his breast, saying, 'God be merciful to me a sinner'. I tell you, this man went down to his house justified rather than the other for everyone that exalteth himself shall be abased (brought down-humbled); and he that humbles himself shall be exalted".

When we receive Jesus as Lord and Savior we receive His power of making us a new creation (II Corinthians 5:17). We are no longer to conform to this world of selfish ideas and ambitions but be transformed by the renewing of our minds (Romans 12:1-2). We let the mind of Christ rule and reign within us which tells us, "But I say unto you, Love your enemies, bless them that curse you, do good to them that hate you, and pray for them that despitefully use you, and persecute you; That ye may be the children of your Father which is in heaven for He maketh His sun to rise on the evil and on the good, and sending rain on the just and the unjust. For if ye love them which love you, what reward have ye? Do not even the publicans the same? And if ye salute your brethren only, what do you more than others? Do not even the publicans so? Be ye therefore perfect (perfect in love-a mature Christian), even as your Father which is in heaven is perfect (God is Love)". I Peter 4:8 exhorts us, "And above all things have fervent charity (love) among yourselves: for charity shall cover a multitude of sins" (See also Proverbs 10:12, I Corinthians 13:4 and James 5:20).

GOD'S VISION OF LOVE FOR WHOSOEVER WILL

Acts 10:9-18 reveal the vision that God gave to Peter to teach him that contrary to the Mosaic Law God has now cleansed all animals for food and that all men are fit for salvation. The vision consisted of a great sheet being let down to earth from haven containing all manner of four-footed beasts of the earth, creeping things and fowls of the air. A voice from heaven told Peter (contrary to the Mosaic Law) to kill and eat. Peter answered that he would not because under the Mosaic Law it was unlawful to eat any food that was considered common or unclean. This was done three times and God answered, "What God hath cleansed, that call not thou common". Then in verse 28 we read, "And he said unto them (those who sent for Paul now in the home of Cornelius, a gentile), 'ye know how that it is unlawful thing for a man that is a Jew to keep company, or come unto one of another nation, but God hath showed me that I should not call any man common or unclean". The message of God is for whosoever will come to Him and receive Jesus as Savior and Lord. God is no respecter of persons.

LOVE: GOD'S BOND OF PERFECTNESS

Of all of God's virtues Love is the one that binds them together in perfect harmony and maturity. Love is God's crowning Grace of Christian perfection (maturity). In Colossians 3:14 we find these Word of grace inspired by God through His Holy Spirit of Truth, "And above all these things (previously mentioned other virtues and fruit of the Spirit) put on charity (love), which is the bond of perfectness". Galatians 5:14 reveals that all of the law and all of the prophetic messages of the prophets of God are summed up in God's Love, "For all the law is fulfilled in one word, even in this: 'thou shalt love thy neighbor as thyself'".

This admonition of God to love our enemies is the same love that we have for our brethren. Galatians 6:10 exhorts us, "As we have therefore opportunity, let us do good unto all men (and women), especially (naturally) unto them who are of the household of faith (Saints of Gods). This includes all those who have received Jesus as Lord and Savior, before, after or during their ordeal of being divorced. Jesus came not to condemn, but to redeem the lost, reconcile them back to God: forgiven, cleansed and restored. Galatians 5:3-4 further states, "For if a man (or woman) thinks himself to be something, when he is nothing, he deceives himself (or herself). But let every man (or woman) prove his (or her) own work (of love), and then shall he (or she) have rejoicing in himself (or herself) alone, and not in another".

The rendition of this Word of God in the Greek New Testament is to help our brothers and sisters in Christ and not consider ourselves to be morally above reproach and thereby have an unscriptural estimate of our own standing before God in Christ. We are not to endeavor to exalt ourselves in the eyes of God by debasing our brethren in Christ. Also, when we haughtily exalt our inflated estimation of our own morality we deceive ourselves and do not the truth. We are to first judge ourselves, prove our own- selves (examine our own works) to see if they be in Christ.

GOD'S REVELATION OF HIS LOVE PERFECTED IN US

First, I John 2 opens with these words of God's Love compassionately spoken to His children, "My little children, these things write I unto you, that ye sin not. And (but) if any man sin, we have an advocate with the Father, Jesus Christ the Righteous; And He is the propitiation (Jesus satisfied God's just demand that sin be punished) for our sins and not for ours only, but also for the sins of the whole world. This includes all sins. Remember that Psalm 51 reveals that all sin is ultimately against God although it may affect other individuals here on earth.

I John 2:3-6 speak to our hearts the Word of God concerning His Love perfected in us, "And hereby we do know that we know Him, if we keep His commandments. He that saith, I know Him, and keepeth not His commandments, is a liar and the truth is not in him. But whoso keepeth His Word in him verily is the Love of God perfected: hereby know we that we are in Him. He that saith he abideth in Him ought himself also so to walk even as He (Christ) walked".

Then in verses 9-13 the Holy Spirit reveals through John, "He that saith he is in the Light (God), and hateth his brother, is in darkness even until now. He that loveth his brother abideth in the light, and there is none occasion of stumbling in him (he does not stumble at the truth neither cause others to stumble). But he that hateth his brother is in darkness, and walketh in darkness, and knoweth not whither he (or she) goeth, because that darkness hath blinded his (or her) eyes". John further expands upon this revelation of truth as recorded in II John 2:5, "And now I beseech thee, lady (one in particular to whom John is writing even though this epistle is also for the benefit of the whole church), not as though I wrote a new commandment unto you (not as if this is a new commandment, only a reminder), but that which we had from the beginning, that we love one another".

CHAPTER NINETEEN

GOD'S INVITATION OF LOVE: COME UNTO ME

LIFE ON EARTH IS TEMPORARY -- ETERNAL LIFE IS FOREVER

The Word of God mentions many sins or lawless behavior of mankind that will keep him or her from passing from this life into eternal life in the Kingdom of God. All of God's created beings will either spend eternity (life after this present life) with God in His dwelling place of joy, peace and rest (God's plan for His most beloved of creation, mankind) or an eternity with the most wicked of all God's created beings, Satan whose aim is to vent his hateful rage and fury upon you in a place that burns with brimstone and fire for all eternity. A place God made for the Devil and his grotesque demons of hell, not for you. However, it is also for those who God will judge on that Great White Judgment Day to be their final eternal home, if they have not received God's remedy for sin: Christ Jesus as Lord and Savior. Make no mistake about it, God's word never returns unto Him void but always accomplishes that for which it is sent and intended. (Isaiah 55:11). God's love and mercy together with His Son, presently our High Priest is evident in this verse, "The Lord is not slack concerning His promise, as some men count slackness; but is longsuffering to usward, not willing that any should perish, but that all should come to repentance. But the day of the Lord will come" (II Peter 3:9-10a). The day of the Lord is the day Jesus returns in judgment as God has given His resurrected and glorified Son's preeminence over all things.

Someday soon, the Lord Jesus will come, "As a thief in the night (when least expected); in which the heavens shall pass away with a great noise, and the elements shall melt, with fervent heat; both the earth and the works that are in it will be burned up (the worlds system of wickedness under Satan). "Therefore, since all these things shall be dissolved, what manner of persons ought you to be in all holy conversation (conduct) and Godliness"(II Peter 3:10b-11).

According to the Word of God, we are in the last age, the last years, the last days and the moment that is seconds before God's midnight hour; the time of His declaring the beginning of the end: the time when Jesus is coming back to receive His redeemed heirs of the Kingdom of God, His Sons and Daughters of Light who are washed in His blood and have endured to the end and are ready to be raptured into the Kingdom of God prepared for His own. Those living at that time shall put on immortality (glorified bodies) and those who have died prior to the rapture shall put on incorruption (glorified bodies); all of whom shall meet Jesus in the air with their spirit man clothed in their new glorified bodies and are transported into Gods place of eternity prepared for His beloved sons and daughters, His children, His family of His Love.

JESUS IS INVITING WHOSOEVER WILL, COME

Jesus is calling today to everyone throughout His created world to come to the Feast of the redeemed, who are seated at a table spread for them in the presence of God the Father and Jesus Christ His Son. You will be attired in the pure white robes of His righteousness which He will provide and receive His special invitation, for all those who qualify, those washed in the blood of the Lamb of God, Jesus Christ the Lord of all.

Whosoever applies to all of God's created beings of all ethnic groups, all races of people, and all cultures: all who are living upon the face of His planet earth. There is no exception, "For God so loved the world that He gave His only begotten Son, that whosoever believeth in Him (Jesus) should not perish, but have everlasting life. For God sent not His son into the world, to condemn the world; but that the world (all people created by the Lord god Almighty through Jesus Christ His Son) through Him might be saved".

In Corinthians 6:9-10, Paul gives a partial list of sins that God abhors and which if anyone has committed God separates Himself from them for they stand guilty of trespasses and sins before a pure and Holy God and are judged to be cast into hell; in fact, "All have sinned and come short of the glory of God" (Romans 3:23). However, even those who throughout the history of this world have committed unmentionable, horrid, wicked, lewd, abominable and murderous sins against their fellow man and ultimately against God, if they with a contrite heart will confess their sins and receive Jesus as Lord and Savior, He will cleanse them from all sin. "For the wages of sin is death: but the gift of God is eternal life through Jesus Christ our Lord" (Romans 6:23).

I Corinthians 6:9-10 states, "Know you not that the unrighteous shall not inherit the Kingdom of God? Be not deceived: neither fornicators (sexually immoral), nor idolaters, nor adulterers, nor effeminate (homosexuals), nor abusers of themselves with mankind, nor thieves, nor covetous, nor drunkards, nor revilers, nor extortioners, shall inherit the Kingdom of God". Now, let's examine this partial list of sins that mankind can and has committed against their fellowman or woman and God.

The Word says that all of God's creation was made in His image, but because they have the will power to choose and Satan has tremendous deceiving powers, many are deceived into disobeying God's law and committing sins against Him. The list begins with fornicators: (Greek porna) which refers to all types and kinds of sexual immorality. It can even mean spiritual fornication (idolatry). Are you a fornicator? Does your life consist as one under the yoke of Satan, bound to live the life of a fornicator or a life of an erotic? Remember, Jesus loves you, not your sin! He is calling all fornicators to come to Him and be washed, cleansed and set free. He will not cast you out. If you will come to Him, He will forgive your sins and wash you in His blood and cleanse you in His pure waters of life. But you must make the decision to repent (turn from) your sin and receive Him and trust Him for your salvation.

Next, Paul refers to idolaters (Greek eidos) an idol or anything (sin) that you worship contrary to the Word of God: You shall not have any other God's before you (between you and God). It also refers to the sinful practices that accompany all kinds of idol worship. Remember, Jesus loves you, not your sin! He is calling all idolaters (those with the lust of the flesh, lust of the eye and pride of life) to come to Him and be washed, cleansed and set free. He will not cast you out. He will forgive you and wash you in His blood and cleanse you in His living waters of life. Again, you must make the eternally significant decision. You must accept His invitation and come to Him and receive Him as Lord and Savior.

Next, the effeminate is mentioned: (Greek moichos); It is feminine and masculine debauchery; It is moral corruption; lustful, perverted adulterous demeanor. Remember, Jesus loves you, not your sin! Jesus is calling all effeminate to come to Him and be washed, cleansed and set free. He will not cast you out. He will forgive you and wash you in His blood and cleanse you in His living waters of life. But, again, you must make the decision. You must make the choice, a life of moral corruption and its wages of eternal death, or receive Jesus as Lord and Savor and trust Him to set you free.

Next, Paul lists abusers of themselves with mankind: (Greek malakos) these are masochists, who derive lustful pleasure from abuse or physical pain; It is a practice of lustful flesh becoming an instrument of lustful desires for their own sinful pleasures. This is a grievous yoke of bondage placed upon an unsuspecting individual who dabbles in this kind of sin. It not only affects the body, but, it establishes strongholds of satanic desires within the mind. But, remember, Jesus loves you, not your sin! He can free you; break the shackles of Satan. If you come to Him and ask, He will not cast you out. He will forgive you; He will cleanse you in His cleansing blood and wash you in His living waters of life.

Paul then refers to those who are thieves: (Greek kleptos) Our English word kleptomaniac refers to someone who habitually steals; one who has an uncontrollable urge to steal. However, this word also is used for thievery that refers to impostors who present themselves as other than what they are in order to thieve from someone else. Perhaps the Identity theft syndrome of today would come under this category. The same word is used in John 10:9-10 when Jesus speaks of Himself as the door of the Sheepfold (the Kingdom of God) and refers to Satan as a thief who presents himself as benefactor of the people whom God created, but in reality comes to steal (kill and destroy) the life that God has given to every man He created. It also refers to any henchmen, cohorts, dupes or deceived slaves of Satan that work in Satan's behalf in this world's system (the principalities, powers and rulers of darkness). Again, Jesus loves you even though your sinfulness separates you from His righteousness. However, Jesus died for your sin and invites you to come to Him (all you who labor for the vanity of this world and are heavy laden with it consequences)! If you will ask, He is faithful and just to forgive you your sins and cleanse you from all unrighteousness.

Another sin mentioned is covetousness: (Greek pleonekteo) an avarice person who defrauds for the sake of gain. It is an inordinate desire to possess by whatever deceitful means necessary to claim what someone else has earned. It is a malady of the mind that provokes one to endeavor to gain the advantage over someone by fraud in order to steal what they have. Jesus is calling, inviting you to give up your vain desires and receive His forgiveness and a life that is more than abundant and free. Jesus pleads that you take His way of life upon you and learn of the benefits of life in Christ Jesus as Lord. He loves you and will never leave you nor forsake you. His grace is sufficient for your every need.

The next sin mentioned is drunkards: (Greek methuo) Referring to those who are intoxicated or drunk with strong drink; whether it is a state of inebriation or an uncontrollable urge sponsored by greed to obtain power by one's own devices: drunk with power. In either case, it is a condition whereby the person so affected loses their common sense and displays irrational behavior. Those of you so disposed remember, Jesus loves you and while there is yet time, invites you to drink of the water of life freely through Him who died for you and receive life everlasting. Jesus loves you, not your sin and in His omniscience He realizes that the enemy of your soul has corrupted your ways and His desire is to reconcile you back into the arms of grace and love and safety and eternal salvation; a state of sanity.

Also in danger of suffering the wrath of God in judgment are revilers (Greek loidoros) which identify those who verbally abuse, malign, deride or vilify someone to their hurt. It is to rail, rant, scold, chide or complain bitterly or abusively against another. When Jesus hung on the cross, the Jews railed at Him and reviled Him, they blasphemed Him as he in excruciating pain hung upon the cross between heaven and earth, but because He loved his created beings so, Jesus prayed, "Father forgive them for they know not what they do" (Luke 23:34). Likewise, Jesus loves you and has given His life for you that whosoever will come to Him and receive Him (Jesus) as Lord and Savior shall be saved: spared the judgment of the wrath of God.

Last in this partial list of those who shall not inherit the Kingdom of God are the extortioners: (Greek harpage) those who unlawfully plunder and pillage rapaciously (greedily existing by feeding on others) voracious, ravenous. They coerce and intimidate others to satisfy their own lustful desires. But Jesus died for even those who would deny others peace and tranquility and happiness in life. Jesus still extends His invitation to them as whosoever, regardless of what you have done, to come unto Him willingly, asking for His forgiveness and repenting of (to turn away from) their sins and receiving Jesus Christ as Lord and Savior.

Then in the next verse, I Corinthians 6:11 says, "And such were some of you: but you are (now) washed, but you are (now) sanctified (separated unto God), but you are (now) justified (declared righteous) in the name of the Lord Jesus, and by the (Holy) Spirit of our God". All of these crimes committed were against mankind, but, Psalm 51 says that all sin is ultimately against God. All sin is the disobedient lawless breaking of His commandments. Therefore it is God's prerogative, God has the right to forgive, to cleanse, to sanctify to make righteous in His sight. This God will do because of His Love for us.

However, make no mistake about it, God as righteous judge must be true to His Word. His word of Love is synonymous with His Word of judgment because He is faithful to His Word to perform it. God desires for all to come to the saving knowledge in Christ; but God will not contaminate His place of purity and righteousness, of Holiness with those who are tainted with sin and who will not come to Him in Jesus Name for forgiveness, cleansing and reconciliation.

FINAL WARNING TO THE FINAL CHURCH DISPENSATION

Jesus speaks to this age recorded in Revelation 3:14-22 and presents Himself as the Amen, the faithful and true witness of God. Amen; because Jesus is the final Word of Truth on things pertaining to the last days. Faithful witness; because Jesus is the Word of God and His Faithful and True witness in fulfilling all the Word of God. Jesus is the beginning of the creation of God or, "In the beginning was the Word, and the Word was with God, and the Word was God. The same was in the beginning with God. All things were made by Him; and without Him (Jesus) there was not anything made that was made" (John 1:1-3).

As God, Jesus is omniscient, therefore He addresses the Laodicean Church, "I know your works, that you are neither cold nor hot (In keeping His word and living for God in Christ): I would you were cold (antichrist) or hot (in Christ). So then because you are lukewarm, and neither cold nor hot, I will spew (vomit) you out of my mouth. Because you say, 'I am rich (estimation of one's accomplishments), and increased with goods, and have need of nothing (not even Christ), how can you not know you are wretched, and miserable, and poor, and blind, and naked (transparent as glass): I counsel you to buy of me gold tried (refined) in the fire (the Holy Spirit baptism), that you may (truly) be rich; and white raiment (robes of righteousness), that you may be properly clothed as becoming my child, and that the shame of your nakedness does not appear, (cannot be discerned by others); and anoint your eyes with eyesalve (anointing ointment), that you may see. As many as I love, I rebuke and chasten (discipline): be zealous (earnestly desires for the things of God) therefore, and repent".

I Peter 4:17-18 warns, "For the time is come that judgment must begin at the house of God: and if it first began at (with) us what shall the end be of them that obey not the gospel of God? And if the righteous scarcely be saved, where shall the ungodly and the sinner appear (in judgment)?" This is true in our life of faith and it is true when the redeemed of the Lord are raptured. They shall be the first to stand before God in judgment, not for our sins, for they are all under the blood of Jesus. For the Saints of God there is no condemnation. However, we will be judged on what we did with our lives in Christ and whether or not our works in Him as His workmanship are considered to be valued even as gold and silver and precious gems. The word says that even though we build upon the only foundation of righteousness that God will accept, Jesus Christ the Lord, our works could resemble, wood, straw or stubble (stumps, stalks, or remnants) if they are not in Christ Jesus (I Corinthians3:11-15).

After the millennial reign of Christ is the resurrection of the dead, who rejected Jesus, God's Christ and then shall be the Great White Throne Judgment for the unsaved, those not found in the book of Life.

There are only two classifications of mankind that God will judge at the end of time: the saved and the unsaved, those who believed God's Word and received Jesus as Lord and Savior and those who rejected the Truth, the Word of Life; referred to and compared as the good seed and the bad seed; the wheat and the tares; the sheep and the goats; the righteous and the ungodly;

Within the second group is a group of people who decided to grasp hold of both worlds. They believe that they can keep one foot in the world system of lust and sin and the other in the congregation of the righteous. The Book of Jude says that they do not the truth and have become false teachers of the Gospel of Christ; they have hidden stains, ungodly men who turn the grace of God into lasciviousness and denying the only Lord God, our Lord and Savior Jesus Christ; they are arrogant and self-righteous; they are clouds without water; unstable and carried about by every wind of folly; trees with withering fruit; twice dead (spiritually and physically); plucked up by the roots (no anchor to their soul because there is no foundation); they are raging and foaming waves that are contrary and are blown to and fro with every wind of controversy; "for whom is reserved the blackness of darkness (hell) forever". They have not heeded the admonition of the Lord to come out from among those who love darkness more than light.

Jesus speaks of these hypocrites in Matthew 7:21-23, "Not everyone that says unto Me, Lord, Lord, shall enter into the Kingdom of Heaven; but he that does the will of my Father which is in heaven. Many will say unto Me in that Day (Day of Judgment), 'Lord, Lord, have we not prophesied (preach and taught) in your name? And in your name have cast out devils (demons)? And in your name (have) done many wonderful works (miracles)?' And then I will profess unto them, I never knew you: depart from me, you that work iniquity".

Not everyone who professes Christ in this world is necessarily in or of Christ; only those who do the will of the Father and receives Jesus as Lord and Savior in their heart (spirit) and have received the earnest (proof) through the presence of the Holy spirit of Truth. Romans 8:9b and 14 says, "Now if any man has not the Spirit of Christ, he is none of His. For as many as are led by the Spirit of God (Christ), they are the children of God". The Holy Spirit of God speaks to our spirit and we know that we have been sealed as His sons and daughters of Light for eternity. We are led, guided, directed, and counseled by His Holy Spirit. We hear what the Holy Spirit says to our hearts and obey His voice. We keep God's commandments and follow after Jesus, the Way, the Truth and the Life.

BE SURE OF YOUR CALLING AND ELECTION

Ii Peter 1:10 exhorts us, "Wherefore the rather, brethren, give diligence (strive earnestly) to make (to confirm, establish, make certain) your calling (an inner commitment, investment and endowment in the Kingdom of Heaven) and election (chosen by Christ as His own elect by His grace) sure (established within eternally): for if ye do these things (walk in the Spirit), ye shall never fall (stumble)".

Matthew 24:13-24 warns, "But he that shall endure to the end, the same shall be saved. And this gospel of the Kingdom shall be preached in all the world for a witness unto all nations; and then shall the end come". In Jesus parable of the sower recorded in Matthew 13:19-23 Jesus speaks of those who hear the Gospel and joyously receive it, however, there is no depth of belief, no deep rooted convictions; they endure for a while and wither away. Tribulation and persecution causes them to be offended and they no longer continue in the faith.

Jesus as recorded in John 6: 39-40 (Amplified Bible) said, "You search and investigate and pore over the Scriptures diligently, because you suppose and trust that you have eternal life through them. And these (very Scriptures) testify about Me! And still you are not willing (but refuse) to come to Me that you may have life".

GOD'S FINAL INVITATION TO THE WORLD

Even in this midnight hour when the Last Trumpet of God shall very soon sound and clearly be heard over all the world by those who are tuned in through His Spirit, Jesus gives this invitation recorded in Revelation 3:20: "Behold, I stand at the door (of your heart) and knock: if any man (whosoever will) hear my voice, and open the door, I will come in to Him, and will sup (spiritually dine) with him, and He with Me".

Then the final sobering invitation that should make all of humanity so concerned about them-selves to take notice and read what saith the Lord God Almighty. "And the (Holy) Spirit and the bride (the church say, Come. And let him that thirsts come. And whosoever will (desires), let him take the water of life freely. For I (Jesus) testify unto every man (humanity) that hears the words of the prophecy of this Book (Bible), if any man shall add unto these things, God shall add unto him the plagues that are written in this book" And if any man (anyone) shall take away from the words of the Book of this prophecy, God shall take away his part out of the Book of Life, and out of the Holy city, and from the things which are written in this Book. He which (Who) testifies (of) these things (Jesus) says, "Surely I come quickly". Amen, even so, come, Lord Jesus.

The prophecy (of the Revelation of Jesus Christ) is sealed by God, the time is at hand. "He that is unjust (act unjustly-deceitful), let him be unjust still: and he which (who) is filthy (morally polluted), let him be filthy still: and he that is righteous, let him be righteous still: and he that is Holy, let him be Holy still. And behold I come quickly" (Revelation 22:11-12).

THE END AND THE BEGINNING

This will be a time of God's Great Family Reunion. "And I saw a new heaven and a new earth: for the first heaven and the first earth were passed away; and there was no more sea. And I John saw the holy city, New Jerusalem, coming down from God out of heaven, prepared as a bride adorned for her husband" (Revelation 21:1-2). This is the description of the eternal state of the redeemed of the Lord. As we are a new creation in Christ Jesus, God has prepared for us a New Heaven and a New Earth. The word for new used her is the Greek Word kainos which refers to the complete renovation, the remaking of the present heaven and earth as a place of higher excellence: to renew, restore, purify and prepare it as a place for His new created beings: those sanctified and purified and separated unto Himself; those who are the redeemed of the Lord.

God is bringing to an end the lawlessness, immorality, wickedness and iniquitous behavior of those without God through Jesus Christ His Messiah. This ushers in a new beginning for the family of God, His elect, those predestinated before the beginning of creation. All things in heaven and earth shall be renewed for this New Beginning. We shall have access to His Kingdom on Earth and His Kingdom in Heaven simultaneously. There is a New Day dawning where old things are passed away and behold, all things are become new!